FINDING GRACE
THROUGH MARY'S EYES

Claire A. Patterson, M.Ed.

LifeRich Publishing is a registered trademark of The Reader's Digest Association, Inc.

LifeRich Publishing books may be ordered through booksellers or by contacting:

LifeRich Publishing
1663 Liberty Drive
Bloomington, IN 47403
www.liferichpublishing.com
844-686-9607

ISBN: 978-1-4897-3166-1 (sc)
ISBN: 978-1-4897-3165-4 (hc)
ISBN: 978-1-4897-3167-8 (e)

Library of Congress Control Number: 2020920729

Print information available on the last page.

LifeRich Publishing rev. date: 11/09/2020

To Chris, Alicia, Michael, and Ella,
who all promise to take care of me,
when I get too feeble to take care of myself.
And to Cody, my biggest fan.

In conformity with the decrees by Pope Urban VIII, the author recognizes and accepts that the final authority regarding the messages presented here-in, rests with the Holy See of Rome, to whose judgement she willingly submits.

Upon the approval of Pope Paul VI, on October 14, 1966, with the abolition of previous Canon 1399 and 2318 of the former Canonical Code, and the decree of the Congregation for the Propagation of the Faith, S.A.S. 58. 1186, publications about new appearances, revelations, prophecies, miracles, etc., have been allowed to be distributed and read by the faithful without the express permission of the Church, providing they contain nothing which contravenes faith and morals. This means that no imprimatur is necessary when distributing information on new apparitions not yet judged or approved by the Church.

In 2003, Father Leroy Smith, from Our Lady of the Holy Spirit Center, assembled a panel of three priests and Gerald Ross. All members of this team were very knowledgeable regarding Marian apparitions. They interviewed Calvin Patterson, Jr. several times over a period of three months. They also examined the messages he had received from Mary prior to that time. They concluded that: "Calvin Patterson and his messages have been affirmed authentic and worthy of instruction." This notice was published in the August/September 2003 edition of the "Our Lady of the Holy Spirit Center Newsletter", volume 10 issue 5. They also published two messages Duke had been given by Mary for "all who will listen" in that edition.

Bible references included in this book have been taken from The New American Bible, Catholic Book Publishing Co. New York

Since 2001, whenever Duke or I would talk to people about our experiences, we were asked to "Write it all down!" So now I have. I hope you experience a special Grace as you read the messages from our Blessed Mother, Jesus and others. Throughout it all, Duke and I always felt the watchful eyes of our Blessed Mother and her Son. Although we faced many challenges, our lives were shaped and protected by their love.

> **"To whomever I send you, you shall go; whatever I command you, you shall speak. Have no fear before them, because I am with you to deliver you, says the Lord."**
>
> **Jer 1: 7b-8**

I would like to extend my deepest gratitude to the following dear friends and family members who read each line and contributed so much. They were fearless in telling me when something should be deleted, changed, or added. They had wonderful ideas and helped to clarify the story line when I got off track or muddled down.

Mary Ann Brausch, Joseph Gering, Terri Lachtrupp, Walter Miller

I would also like to humbly thank those who pray for me and the readers of this book.

Contents

1

Opposites Attract

Calvin Stanley Patterson Jr. (called Duke since he was an infant) was born in June 1950 in Cincinnati, Ohio. His parents were Calvin and Rosemary. They were both from working class families and experienced a life of poverty in their early years.

Calvin Sr. had been in both the navy and the marines during the first years of their marriage. According to Rosemary, Calvin was a kind and loving husband until he returned from fighting in Korea. Something happened there that caused him to suffer bouts of anxiety, depression, and unexplained anger. His behavior became unpredictable.

Sometimes he would beat Duke for very little provocation; other times he would remain calm when there was a reason to be angry. Duke told me that when he was a teenager, he came home once after a car accident and expected his father to hit the roof. Instead, his dad said, "Things happen. Don't worry about it." In his fifties Calvin Sr. became a deacon in the Seventh-Day Adventist church and seemed to settle down, but he was still prone to unaccountable fits of temper.

Rosemary was a hard-working, God-loving woman. She and Calvin Sr. (Chad to friends) had three children—Calvin Jr. (Duke), Judith Ann in 1956, and Ronald Allen in 1958. She converted to the Seventh-Day Adventist church around 1956. Through her influence, Duke attended a Seventh-Day Adventist school from the first grade through the tenth grade. His siblings also attended the school for a short time. Rosemary worked full time for many years to help support the family and pay for their private school education. She also battled chronic back pain, cancer, and Parkinson's disease. I remember wondering why such a loving and kind woman would be faced with so many challenges. She was a great role model for me on how to deal with difficulties in life and still keep a positive attitude.

When Duke was twelve, he became very ill with an infection and was hospitalized for a week. He was near death at one point when a large angel appeared in his room. Duke was very frightened. The angel told Duke that he had come to take him away, but somehow the plan had changed and that it was not his time to die. Then the angel left as quickly as he had arrived. This was not the first time Duke came close to death. Many years later we laughed about how often his guardian angel had to work overtime to keep him alive.

Duke finished his high school years in a public school. At that point he stopped following the Seventh-Day Adventist life-style, which included a vegetarian diet and sobriety. He enrolled in the University of Cincinnati in the pre-med program in 1968 but got caught up in the party scene, and his grades suffered. He began smoking and drinking when he was eighteen. He struggled with alcoholism until he was thirty-four years old, when he became a recovering alcoholic and never drank again.

Duke left college after two years and joined the navy after his father became angry over his grades. The navy solved two problems for Duke: he got away from home, and he didn't have to worry about being sent to fight in the jungles of Vietnam.

Shortly before he left for boot camp in January 1971, Duke and I met. We were each dating other people at the time, but the attraction was strong. When Duke came home on leave in March 1971, we had our first date.

He was stationed in San Francisco for a couple of years and then transferred to Puerto Rico. He had three brushes with death during his time on the island. The first was when he and his buddies took out a rubber raft to visit a nearby island. An unexpected storm blew in. They were bailing water with their hands, and the raft had been punctured and was losing air. They all thought they were going to drown.

Another time he was swimming at a place called "Crash-Boat Beach". He was sucked out to sea by the strong undertow and managed to climb up on a rock until someone could come out and rescue him with a boat.

A third time he was swimming in the ocean and was attacked by a man-of-war. He was in the hospital for a week and carried the scars from this misadventure all of his life.

Perhaps Satan wanted him to die while he was living a less than prayerful life, but God continued to save him for a reason.

I was born in December 1950 in Cincinnati, Ohio. My parents were Ruth and Lloyd. Ruth had worked as a secretary for ten years before they got married. Lloyd had served in the navy during World War II and then worked a variety of jobs. He eventually settled into a career in sales for the rest of his life. I had three younger brothers, David, Jeff, and Tom.

Mom was a devout Catholic. She taught me my first prayers when I was very young and bought a series of books for me about the saints. She taught me about her favorite saint, St. Therese of Lisieux, and she became my favorite saint also. My mother was basically a stay-at-home mom, but she worked part-time jobs to support our Catholic education. My brothers and I all attended Catholic schools from first through twelfth grades.

Mom suffered from lupus the last nineteen years of her life. She was in a lot of pain and partially disabled much of that time. It was particularly hard for her because my youngest brother, Tom, was only two years old when she began to experience symptoms of the disease. So, in addition to the pain, she felt inadequate as a mother. However, since she could not do things physically with her youngest, they had a lot of great conversations. Again, I wondered why such a good person would have to suffer so much.

My father had converted to Catholicism shortly before they were married and attended Sunday mass with our family, but he was not part of my religious education. Dad was a good father, and he worked very hard to support us—usually twelve-hour days. He was also involved in our sports activities. In his later years, we heard stories about his experiences during World War II. After retiring, he enjoyed visiting schools and sharing his stories as well. He loved our country and would get upset when people disrespected the American flag and everything it stood for.

When I was about nineteen years old, I began to think about joining the Carmelite religious order, partly because I had a devotion to St. Therese, the Little Flower. I didn't think I would have any problem with the vows of poverty, chastity, and obedience, and the contemplative life seemed very attractive. I dated a few guys in college but no one seriously. As I was sending out inquiring letters to some convents, I met and fell in love with Duke.

Our romance was a long-distance one involving many letters and audio tapes. Duke proposed on July 14, 1972, and we were married at St. Theresa of Avilla Church in Cincinnati on July 14, 1973. I did not notice, but several people told me later that as we were saying our vows, there was a thunderstorm. This could be interpreted two ways: God was not happy with our union, or He was clapping his hands with joy. I like to believe it was the latter.

2

Newly Married

Duke and Claire, July 14, 1973.

Duke was stationed on a navy and air force base in Puerto Rico at the time we were married, so we flew there for our new life together. In some ways it was wonderful. We were on an island paradise, living in base housing near beautiful beaches. Our house was furnished, and we had a yard with fruit trees.

I had recently graduated with a degree in education and found a job right away teaching in a Baptist mission school. It was a very small school with grades K–12. There were only four teachers—the Baptist minister, his wife, another navy wife, and me. We all taught multiple grades. I had grades three through six, which consisted of thirteen children. The kids were all very dear to me, and I hated leaving them when Duke was transferred to another base.

I attended mass each Sunday in a small church on a hill overlooking a beach. Duke had no interest in coming to church with me, but he never discouraged me from going. Sometimes I suggested we pray together, but he expressed his belief that prayer was personal between God and him. He did not feel comfortable praying with others, not even with me.

We did not have a TV, radio, or much money, so we played a lot of cards and board games, went to the base movie theater (tickets were thirty-five cents each), and had long talks getting to know each other.

One memorable conversation was about hitchhiking. I told Duke that as a driver, I had never picked up a hitchhiker, but my girlfriends and I did once. My friend, Connie, was the first to drive and the first to have access to a car. It was a convertible! During the summer of 1968, there were five of us in her car driving around Cincinnati with the top down. We saw this cute blonde guy in shorts hitchhiking, and for a lark, we talked Connie into stopping for him. There was no room for him to sit, so we told him he would have to lie across our laps in the back seat. He said he didn't mind at all and got in. I remember him lying on his back with his head in my lap. We just giggled until he got out. As Duke listened to this story, his jaw dropped. "That was me! That was the only time I ever hitchhiked! My car had broken down, and I needed a lift home. I remember lying in the back seat and the girls just laughing the entire trip!"

In January of 1974, Duke was transferred to the Norfolk Naval Base in Virginia. Our first furnished apartment was a short walk from a Catholic church and school. As it was mid-school year, I applied for a substitute teaching job. The principal offered me a teaching position with five students at substitute pay. (fifteen dollars per day in those days) These five girls were in seventh and eighth grades and had been suspended until the end of the year for buying marijuana. Their parents had petitioned the school for in-school suspension, and, when I showed up, a solution presented itself.

We were assigned to an unused wing of the school and I taught them all subjects of their curriculum. It was another unique and wonderful job. I was offered a full-time job teaching fifth grade the following year.

Because of my proximity to church and school, I could attend daily mass. We only needed one car, and very little else. We enjoyed trips to the local gardens and beaches. We developed great friendships with the teachers at the school as well as the local parish priest, Father Jim. It was the first time Duke was surrounded by a lot of Catholics and got to know a priest as a friend. It helped him become comfortable with a culture of prayerful and joyful people.

Duke and I were encouraged by Fr. Jim to make a Marriage Encounter weekend. We did this in April 1975. It was a wonderful, Spirit-filled weekend for both of us. We learned so much about spousal communication and how to involve God in our relationship. Christopher Allen, our first child, was born nine months after this weekend.

In looking back, we were sometimes protected by angels, even though we didn't know it at the time. We made our first trip to visit family in Cincinnati, after Chris was born, when he was only two months old. Back then we didn't have money for hotels, so we made the twelve-hour drive straight through. We couldn't leave home until Duke had returned from work, so we were driving throughout the night. We were somewhere in the Tennessee mountains, along a winding two-lane road, when we realized we were heading in the wrong direction. Duke tried making a U-turn, but ended up going off the road into a ditch. It was near 1:00 a.m. and pitch dark. As we were counting our money and realizing we didn't have enough for a tow, (even if we could somehow locate a tow-truck) we saw two cars pull to the side of the road above us. Nine strong-looking young men came down the hill and, with me steering and Duke helping to push, got us back on the road. Duke took out his wallet to pay them something for their help and they vanished. We guessed they had been angels, but were never sure until years later, when Our Blessed Mother confirmed it to Duke during one of their conversations.

Duke left the navy after six years of service in December 1976. We moved back to Cincinnati into a small apartment. The next two years were the worst years of our lives. We both made very little money and Duke was drinking a lot.

At some point around 1977, Duke was making four dollars and fifty cents per hour working in electronics. His father told him, in front of me and his mother, that he was not a "real man" if he didn't support his family with at least two hundred and fifty dollars per week. I saw Duke shrink into himself in utter humiliation. Throughout the rest of his life, his father insulted him in hurtful ways.

Duke had a terrible car accident while driving home drunk one night in 1978. He hit a telephone pole head-on. When he looked at the car the next day, he realized that he should have died in that accident, but he had walked out without a scratch. That woke him up to the fact that he was an alcoholic, and he promised to stop drinking. He did so for the next six years.

I was teaching in a private Hebrew Day school at that time, and making less than half what I could make in the public schools. I dearly loved the kids and my job, but we had decided to start saving for a house. After teaching there for three years, I regretfully handed in my resignation, and took a job in the public-school system. We were able to buy a small house in Greenhills, Ohio shortly after that.

In August 1980, I completed my master's degree in Educational Administration, and was offered a great job with a large school district.

Our daughter, Alicia Marie, was born in May 1981.

Duke had been working hard and earning promotions, and our financial situation was stabilizing. The missing piece in our family was that the children and I attended Sunday Mass without Duke. I prayed silently for Duke's conversion, but it was a topic we never discussed.

In 1984, Duke was thirty-four years old and had been promoted into a job in the purchasing department with a large company. His colleagues routinely visited a bar each afternoon before heading home from work. Duke didn't want the men to think he was a wimp or anti-social, so he went with them. He decided that since he was an adult with two children, he could control his drinking. Of course, he couldn't, and he came home drunk many evenings. I told him that if this didn't stop, he would lose me and children. At that point he stopped drinking for the rest of his life.

Outside of his drinking, Duke was a wonderful, loving, and generous husband and father. He was not only generous to us, but he helped anyone who asked him for anything. He would often bring milk to his sister for her family and pay her electric bills. He helped her children when they needed assistance. He helped other members of the family, and even strangers, whenever they asked for it. He never expected any pay-backs; he was always happy to give. If a kid came to the door selling anything, he always bought it.

I remember one Saturday, Duke took four boys, who didn't have fathers in their lives, to the Cincinnati Zoo. I stayed home cleaning the house, mowing the grass, paying the bills, and generally resenting him for leaving me with all of the work. I even went to confession to talk to a priest about how I felt. He reminded me of Lazarus' sisters, Martha and Mary. He said Duke was acting like Mary (sitting at the feet of Jesus) and I was acting like Martha (complaining), and I should try to be more like him.

In 1986, while visiting my mother, we watched a program together about the events occurring in Medjugorje. According to the reporter, the Blessed Mother had been appearing to six children in this small village in Yugoslavia since 1981. This was a real revelation to me. I had only heard about apparitions in Fatima and Lourdes. As a child I had watched movies about those events. I thought they were the only two times in history that Our Blessed Mother had appeared to anyone. My mother and I were enthralled with the program and amazed that Our Lady could be appearing in our life-time. We talked about going there together, but it was not a realistic goal, given mom's poor health, and my children and job responsibilities. The idea of going to that special little village, however, was planted in my heart and soul, and would persist for years.

Each time after that, when Duke would bring up the subject of our next vacation, I would suggest going to Medjugorje. My idea got shot down rather quickly, however, and we usually ended up at a beautiful beach somewhere.

One hallmark of our marriage was when we attended a second Marriage Encounter weekend in 1988. This weekend had a tremendous impact on our relationship with each other and with God. I really felt the Holy Spirit moving within us. We joined a "circle" immediately following the weekend, and also became circle and zone leaders. We seemed to be on fire with the Holy Spirit. We began praying as a couple, which we had never done before, and we were communicating on a more loving, deeper, and beneficial manner. All of the members of our circle were Catholics with similar values, and it gave Duke more exposure to Catholic life among our newly-found friends. Encouraged by a member of our circle, I began saying a five-decade rosary each morning, and as a family, we began reading the bible after dinner each night.

Duke and Claire are walking in a community parade with their Marriage Encounter circle banner.

At some point in late 1989, Duke and I attended a Marriage Encounter leadership meeting, where our challenge was to pray to the Holy Spirit to help us write a letter to our spouse from God. This might sound hokey, but we took it seriously, and it was the first time the curtain lifted, when Jesus spoke through Duke. I have two letters I treasure.

Here is the first letter to me:

"My Gentle Child.

I'm so pleased with your daily devotion and your desire to walk with me.

It delights my heart to see the love you hold in your heart for our Father.

10

When you are tired, sad or weary, I will always be there to lift you up. You are my precious sister through God's infinite love. I am your devoted big Brother.

It gives me delight to watch your interaction with your children and your husband. It pleases me more than you'll ever know when you insist that they spend time with me.

In turn, I have blessed you above others. I have given you your family, your health, and peace of heart. I love you dearly.

I am looking forward to the time when we can spend eternity walking and talking together.

All My love, Jesus"

This is my second letter:

"My Sweet Child,

It is wonderful to be able to talk [to you] again. I wish that we could take more time to just talk. I love you so very much; more than you can imagine. I want you to know my love on a personal level.

I take such joy in the compassion and concern you display for my children.

You are my little flower. Please come to me and let's walk together and talk together.

Love, Jesus"

The reference to the "little flower" in the second letter struck my heart. Any devotee of St. Therese of Lisieux knows that she wished to be a little flower in God's garden. That was my wish also, but I never shared this with Duke until I read this letter.

Mom died in November 1989, and it was devastating for me. She was my only confidant regarding so many things, especially my faith. Duke never criticized me for my religious beliefs, but he couldn't understand them. When I attended a Good Friday service alone in 1987, and felt especially moved by Our Blessed Mother's loss and suffering, I cried all the way home. I felt so close to Our Blessed Mother that night. I called my mom and shared the experience with her. Duke would never have understood the depths of my feelings at that time.

In 1990, after experiencing promotions and regular increases in our salaries, Duke suggested we move from our modest home in Greenhills and build a new home in a nicer neighborhood. I resisted for about a year, but he finally wore me down. A big part of his motivation for this move was to prove to his father, and perhaps my father also, that he was a good provider for his family. Believing that material and financial success was the most important way to prove his manhood, his self-worth was dependent upon the possession of high-priced things. In addition to the new big house, he bought me expensive gifts, took his family on nice vacations, and bought himself a new sports car. I was resistant to all of these purchases, but got overruled rather quickly.

In the late 1980's through the 1990's I was struggling with my own battles of pride and humility. It wasn't so much about money for me, as it was about status and control. I continued to seek promotions within the school district. I realized many years later that this was a sin of pride, and a sin of neglecting my family. I worked very long days and often Saturdays. My faith and family were coming in a distant second and third to my career and ambitions.

In 1996, Chris was twenty years old and majoring in Spanish. He decided to spend part of his summer in a Spanish-speaking country, and picked Costa Rica. I told him to call me once a week, collect, so I would know he was okay. When he arrived and settled into the youth hostel in San Jose, he called. Then I didn't hear from him again for forty-four days! (Yes, I was keeping track!) I began having nightmares about what was happening to him. I called the American Embassy in San Jose and reported him missing. I didn't know what else to do.

During that time, I was on our deck, putting down a fresh coat of varnish. As I painted, I prayed the rosary. When I got to the Fifth Joyful Mystery, (finding the Christ Child in the temple) I began having a conversation with Mary. "You know what it's like. You lost your twelve-year old Son for three days. You were worried, as I am now. Please help us."

Then, I noticed a beautiful monarch butterfly sitting on the deck near where I was painting. As I worked my way toward the butterfly, I kept expecting it to fly away, but it just stayed there until I was right next to it. Suddenly, the butterfly hopped up, touched my lips and flew away. I felt a sense of peace and relief. I knew that Our Lady had sent this butterfly to ease my anxiety and let me know that Christopher was all right. Chris told me later that he had been robbed twice, after he called me the first time, and was afraid that if he called and told me about his mishaps, I would worry. Ha! He had no notion of how a mother worries! I appreciated Mother Mary's concern and comfort when I most needed it. I didn't share any of this experience with Duke. I thought if I told him Mary had sent a butterfly to kiss me, and because of that, I knew Chris was safe, he would just laugh.

The 1990's brought us better incomes, but less peace. Duke was having frequent migraines and went to a few doctors for relief. They did a number of tests, but couldn't find a source for the headaches. He started taking pain pills so he could function. I was focused on work, and didn't have a lot of sympathy for him. I usually reported to my school building by 6:30 a.m. and didn't leave until 5:00 p.m. I frequently took work home for the evenings. I didn't attend daily Mass and hadn't been to confession for years. Even with Marriage Encounter holding us together, we were heading down a dangerous path.

3

An Eventful Year

1999 was an important year for us is many ways. In January of that year, I finally persuaded Duke to agree to a family trip to Medjugorje. I put eight hundred dollars down as a deposit for the four of us to go in June of 1999. A few weeks later, we were watching the news, and saw people fleeing Croatia in a panic. Duke became concerned about our safety, and insisted that I cancel our trip. So, through tears of disappointment, I did. My son, Chris, sent me a lovely letter from college saying that he believed Our Lady would keep us safe and that we should still go on the pilgrimage. Duke was immovable on the subject.

In March of 1999, I made a Christ Renews His Parish weekend at St. John the Evangelist Church in West Chester, Ohio. This was a very emotional and faith-filled experience, and I found a few important friends with the same values. Some of us began meeting for rosary once a week, and the entire group met regularly for the next six months, as we prepared to present a weekend in September. Those months were a source of tremendous growth in my spiritual life. I felt my Blessed Mother calling me to Medjugorje even stronger than ever.

In April of 1999, one of my CRHP sisters, Mary Ann, gave the St. Louis de Montfort consecration book to me. I completed my consecration to Jesus through Mary on May 31, The Feast of the Visitation. Things in our lives began to change rapidly after that.

In June of 1999, after almost 26 years of marriage, Duke told me that he wanted to become a Catholic. I asked him how he had finally reached this decision. He said that after eleven years of Catholic Marriage Encounter involvement, he was desirous for more participation in the faith. I'm sure that this was a gift to me from Mary and Jesus following my consecration. Duke and my son, Christopher, started The Right of Christian Initiation for Adults (RCIA) classes that September, and I attended with them. It just so happened that Mary Ann, who had given the consecration prayer book to me, was sponsoring a confirmation candidate at the same time. So, she attended each RCIA class with us. God's hand was evident in this.

Duke had been tormented with migraine headaches since about 1984, but in 1999 he also experienced pain in his hands. One doctor traced both problems to a pinched nerve in his neck. In the summer of 1999, Duke underwent surgery that involved taking part of the bone from his hip and inserting it into his neck. That did not eliminate the headaches, but it did alleviate the pain in his hands.

In August, Jeanie, a friend of the family, who had traveled to Medjugorje in the early 1990's, invited me to a special event at Our Lady of the Holy Spirit Center (OLHSC) in Norwood, Ohio. She told me that Our Blessed Mother was scheduled to appear there on the evening of August 31. I had never heard of OLHSC, but was eager to go. Duke did not consider going, as he didn't believe that Our Blessed Mother could appear to anyone. Having grown up with the Seventh-Day Adventist teachings, he believed that when anyone died, including Our Blessed Mother, they remained "asleep" and unaware of anything on earth or in heaven.

I wasn't sure what to expect, but as I drove near OLHSC about 7:00 p.m. on August 31, I saw crowds of people walking up a hill carrying lawn chairs and blankets. I parked as close as I could get, in a CVS parking lot about a half-mile away. I knew that my friend was waiting for me somewhere in the crowd of about twenty thousand people (as reported in the newpaper the next day). I had just begun walking down one of the driveways on the property, when I heard Jeanie call my name. That was my first small miracle of the evening; the fact that we found each other so quickly amidst so many people.

Jeanie gave me a tour through the building, pointing out special statues, including one that had reportedly wept. She also showed me where confessions were being held on the porch of the former Bishop's residence. I decided to get into a line for confession. As I waited and prayed, I noticed flashes of light over one priest's head. I remember thinking that it was very rude, intrusive, and inconsiderate of someone to take photos of those confessing. I stayed in line, took my turn, and returned to my friend.

Later, there was a procession of the Blessed Sacrament under a canopy. As it neared us, we knelt in honor of Our Lord. Again, I noticed flashes of light under the canopy. This time I thought, "How disrespectful! They should be adoring Jesus instead of taking photos."

As I had worked all day in my school district, and was scheduled to work the next morning (which meant a 5:45 a.m. wake-up), I began wondering how much later this night would go on before Our Blessed Mother came as promised. However, I was not about to leave before the big event. Time passed quickly as we prayed the rosary, attended holy mass, prayed the Divine Mercy Chaplet, and listened to sacred music.

Shortly before midnight, someone on a loud speaker said that all of the lights on the outside and inside of the building would be turned off. They requested that no one use flash photography. As soon as everything became dark, I began to see sparks around the top of the building. Again, I thought that perhaps people were in the top floor or on the roof taking pictures. Then Jeanie said excitedly, "It's starting! She's coming!" I told her I had seen those sparks earlier. The sparks increased in intensity and frequency all around us --- in the tops of the surrounding trees and bouncing off the sides of the building. It was like watching a light show, only I knew that it was Our Lady's light show. At one point, there seemed to be a large ball of light passing through me. It was like a warm breeze had gone through my body. It was comforting and marvelous. I don't know what the sparks were, or the ball of light was. I only know that it was all a gift from God, and I will be forever grateful.

Then, even while the sparks continued, Father Smith got on a loud speaker from somewhere in the dark, and said that Our Blessed Mother and Jesus had been with us and had delivered a message for us through the Batavia Visionary. Fr. Smith said that Our Lady had requested we sing her favorite song, "Silent Night." We all began singing and waving white handkerchiefs to signal our love for our Mother, just like I had seen in videos of Fatima. I was crying tears of joy. It was truly a wonderful night. Even though I got home after 1:30 a.m., I woke up refreshed and alert for work the next day. I never suffered in any way for not getting my usual eight hours of sleep. I didn't share much of this with Duke at the time. I didn't think he would understand.

I had been reading everything I could about Medjugorje that year, and since I felt such a strong call to go, I wanted to be spiritually prepared for the trip, whenever it happened. I began the "Medjugorje Fast" in December 1999. I had read that Our Blessed Mother recommended this fast to help our prayers become more efficacious. So, I drank only water and ate only bread each Wednesday and Friday. It was a difficult fast for me at first, because I was used to several cups of coffee each day, and I like to eat! I would get severe headaches from lack of caffeine, on top of becoming weak from lack of food. I weaned myself off of caffeine quickly to avoid the headaches. Prayer and multi-grain bread helped with the hunger. I also began attending 6:30 a.m. Mass each day before work, and saying a daily fifteen-decade rosary before sleeping each night.

To top off this wonderful year, Duke and Christopher (then twenty-four) were confirmed in the Catholic Faith at the Easter Vigil Mass in 2000. It was one of the happiest days of my life.

4

Our Blessed Mother Leads Us to Grace

I continued to encourage Duke to travel to Medjugorje with me, but I informed him that I was prepared to go alone or with one of my CRHP sisters. He finally agreed to go, but only to protect me from getting lost or shot by a sniper. This time the trip was to be just the two of us, since our children were involved with their jobs.

Duke still held onto some of the lessons of his youth; specifically, that when a person dies, they are asleep until the second coming of Christ. If I said something like, "I hope Mom sees this from heaven." He would respond with, "You know I don't believe she can see anything. No one is in heaven except God and some of the Old Testament prophets." So, he couldn't conceive of Mary being in heaven or able to visit the earth and talk to six children in Medjugorje. He thought Fatima and Lourdes were hoaxes also. He believed that the children were making up stories for money or attention.

When I mentioned other phenomena, such as rosaries turning gold and the sun spinning, he said that the rosaries were probably made in the village using a special metal, and that when rubbed, changed to a golden color. He was going on this trip to keep me safe, and with many doubts about the authenticity of the events. He would not read any of the material I had, or in any other way prepare for the trip. He was a very stubborn man!

I scheduled our trip for July 7 – 15, 2001, crossed my fingers and toes and prayed and prayed that Our Lord and Our Blessed Mother would touch him in a special way. I prayed that I would not experience any miracles. I wanted to be the one Jesus referred to as, "Blessed are those who have not seen but have believed." I wanted all of the miracles to be given to Duke.

I told Duke bits and pieces of the information I had read, but he was usually reticent to hear much. He did express two concerns about what I had shared with him, based on his knowledge of the Bible. I had mentioned that Mary comes to Medjugorje as the "Queen of Peace," and as such, asks us to pray for peace. He stated that the Bible says there will never be peace on the earth, "So, why would she want us pray for that?" His second concern was that Mary had asked us to consecrate ourselves and our children to her. Duke quoted John 14:6 when Jesus said, **"No one comes to the Father except through Me,"** and that it would be wrong to consecrate our hearts to Mary. I didn't have an answer for him, but suggested that we ask a priest or visionary those questions when we got there.

On July 3, 2001, four days before our scheduled departure, Duke took me outside on our deck after supper to talk. He asked me, for the first time, to tell him more about the visionaries in Medjugorje. I was eager to tell him everything I knew about the six visionaries, and then I mentioned that there were also two locutionists. I began to describe what that meant, and he stopped me and said, "I had a dream last night." He said that Mary had talked to him about 2:00 am that morning. Her first words to him were, "You're so silly." And then she laughed. He said he felt like a small child who was being teased and caressed by his loving mother. He said the peaceful feeling was the same a baby would feel when drawn close to his mother's heart. Mary told him that the words sometimes get mixed up when interpreters translate her messages. She meant that we should consecrate ourselves to God's message. Mary said that she is just a human soul like we are and she is only here by God's Will and Grace. Mary also said that she asks us to pray for peace to lessen the wars and hardships, but there will always be wars. She explained to him why peace is so important to each person, each family, each nation and the world. Mary told Duke that he had a good heart and Jesus is pleased with the way he took care of his children. She said he should open his heart to the Holy Spirit. Our Blessed Mother convinced him that what was happening in Medjugorje was real.

I listened quietly, without interrupting, and when he was finished talking, I said, "I don't think that was a dream." I asked him if I could share this with our son and daughter, and he said, rather emphatically, "NO! Don't say a word to anyone." He said he wasn't even going to share it with me initially. I promised I wouldn't share anything he had told me about his "dream." I did say a prayer of thanksgiving, that Mary had already started touching his heart.

Traveling to Medjugorje is never easy. We left Cincinnati in the afternoon of Saturday, July 7, and arrived in Chicago after a bumpy ride. Some people on the plane had been very worried, but I felt sure that Mary would keep us safe. I believed that Satan was trying to scare me or at least add stress to my experience. As soon as I told the evil one to give up, and that Mary was in charge of this trip, the shaking stopped.

I did not sleep at all during the overnight trip across the ocean. I said a few rosaries and tried to rest. We landed in Zurich where we met other members of our pilgrimage group, including our priest and spiritual director for the trip, Father Bill. It was a very confusing airport and we were given the wrong directions to our connecting gate, but we made it just in time. Father Bill had had the same turbulence on his plane ride, and we discussed how Satan was trying to disrupt our peace. He said a short exorcist prayer as we boarded our next flight to Split, Croatia.

When we arrived in Split, we claimed our bags and found our driver. Then we took a three-hour bus ride to Medjugorje.

We arrived at the boarding house of the Bandic family at 5:50 p.m. on Sunday, July 8. We were led to a very small room, adjacent to Father Bill's room. We shared a small hot water tank with him, and he asked us not to take long showers! Our room contained a small end table between twin beds. We had a tiny shower, with no curtain. The first time I took a shower, I faced the wrong way and ended up spraying the room with water!

It was a rustic house without screens in the windows. Our choice, during those hot summer nights, was to endure the heat or the mosquitoes! Fortunately, I had packed a tube of hydrocortisone cream, which we shared with Father Bill.

We rushed to put our things into our room and then raced to St. James Church, a short walk away, for the 6:00 p.m. Croatian Mass. The Mass was held outside at the back of the church. There were thousands of people and perhaps 60 priests concelebrating on the outdoor altar under a canopy. Many people stayed after mass, kneeling on the concrete for the Croatian prayers.

Our group met at Mary's statue in front of church after Mass. Most people were quietly praying while we walked back to our house. As we had dinner that night, Father Bill shared with us that he had seen the sun turn blue and spin during Mass. None of the rest of us had seen that phenomenon that night. We were all so tired by then, all we wanted to do was crawl upstairs and into our beds.

On Monday, July 9, I woke up at 2:00 a.m. and said two rosaries in the dark. The sun began to rise about 4:30 a.m. I lay in bed peacefully listening to the sounds of dogs barking and roosters crowing. By 5:00 a.m. it was bright enough to record these events in my journal. I began to get the idea of inviting friends to our house when we got home, to share our experiences during our pilgrimage. I wrote in my journal, "I'm not sure how Duke will feel about that."

Duke woke up at 7:00 a.m. and told me that Mary had spoken to him about 3:00 a.m. that morning. She said, "My Angel, I am very happy you are here. I am crying tears of joy." Then she kissed him on the forehead. Duke said it was the most wonderful feeling of love he had ever experienced. He didn't have adequate words to describe what had happened to him.

That morning we attended the 10:00 a.m. English Mass inside the church. After Mass and lunch, we decided to separate for private prayer. Duke walked to the white statue of Mary outside of the church. He stood before the crucifix that was attached to the gate that surrounded the statue. He said that he saw blood on the crucifix, but after praying about ten minutes, the blood disappeared.

While Duke was in the front of the church, I was walking behind the church to see the statue of the risen Jesus. I noticed a young man there, possibly eighteen years of age, kneeling in the sharp rocks as he adored Jesus. (That area is now paved.) I was very moved by his devotion. I have never had the courage to sustain that kind of pain voluntarily. Earlier that morning, I was thinking of how the bare wooden kneelers in the church would cause me pain. Now, I was witnessing a true pilgrim at prayer. That evening, Duke said he may have seen the same young man praying before the statue of the Blessed Virgin in front of the church.

We were told that Mary would appear to Ivan, one of the six visionaries, at 10:00 p.m. on Apparition Hill that night. So, after dinner, we began walking toward the hill about 8:30 p.m. Duke told me that as we approached the hill, he saw a blue light in the sky, and then he saw the whole hill glow with a blue light. (There was no electricity on the hill at that time.) He also saw sparks in the trees, as I had seen on August 31, 1999, at OLHSC. I told him that I did not notice either of these phenomena. He couldn't understand why he could see it and I could not. I told him that it was a gift from God, and he should just relax and enjoy it!

There were estimates of ten thousand pilgrims on Apparition Hill that night. I was amazed at how people reached out their hands to help strangers climb the hill. English was a minority language, but that didn't stop anyone from communicating love! We climbed until the crowd stopped moving and tried to find a flat rock to sit on. We ended up standing, and balancing on sharp rocks, as people were pretty closely packed. At times, folks were singing hymns and playing guitars. Then someone led the rosary in Croatian using the loud speaker. When the music and praying stopped, the only sounds we heard were birds singing. (By the way, birds don't typically sing at 10:00 p.m.) It was a peaceful, holy, and joyful experience with thousands of strangers, in the dark, on a rocky hillside. Where else in the world can one experience such an evening?

We had been told that we would meet with Ivan the next day to hear the message Mary had given him that night. My prayer that evening was that when we met Ivan, he would have a message for me from Mary about my mother. Were they together in heaven? We climbed back down the hill in the dark with the help of flashlights and strangers' strong arms. On the way back to our house, Father Bill said that he had seen lights sparkling in the trees during the apparition, just as Duke had seen. We went straight to bed, exhausted and exhilarated.

Duke told me later, that about 2:00 a.m. Tuesday morning, Our Blessed Mother spoke to him again. She told him that she was just a peasant girl who said "Yes" to God. She said that we should focus on Jesus and that we do not have much time to convert. She said that this is a special time of Grace. She also gave him the following message, which contains some dialogue between them.

"My Angel,

I send you my motherly love and blessings."

I [Duke] could sense in her voice great sorrow. It actually caused my heart to ache, so I asked, "Why are you so sad?"

Mary responded, "Because so few of my children are living my messages. Consecrate your hearts to my Son. Pray for the Holy Spirit to come into your hearts so that my Son can present you before the throne of Grace as a perfect gift. Pray to my Son. Talk to Him. He will bear your burdens and give you strength. If you are being tempted by Satan and feel yourself becoming weak, call on my Son and Satan will flee! I tell you the truth, my angel, Satan is a coward at heart."

I [Duke] said, "Should I tell the others in our group this message?"

Our Lady said, "No, that is not what I desire. [That is not enough.] Tell all who will listen."

I [Duke] said, "But people will say that I'm crazy or a fanatic. Or worse yet, they'll say that I'm a liar."

Our Lady said, "So, look what they did to my Son! Those who have my Son in their hearts will listen. Pray for those who do not."

I [Duke] said, "But why me? I'm so new to the Faith. I have so many doubts and questions!"

Our Lady said, "Yes, I know. You are searching and seeking the truth. You have the heart of a child. You must never lose that heart. You have a good heart, but it needs many prayers. If you do as I have asked, my Son will pour out blessings and graces that you will barely be able to receive! Thank you, for I know that you love your Mother, and you will respond to my call."

Duke had written these remarks on a piece of notebook paper that I had packed for my journaling. I encouraged him to share this message with our group at dinner that evening. That was the usual time we talked about what had happened to us during the day. He was terrified of the prospect and said something like, "I'll think about it."

That same morning, after prayers on the balcony of our house with Father Bill, we had breakfast. Then, we walked to the hall where Ivan was presenting. There were at least three hundred people in the hall at that time. Ivan spoke through an interpreter as he shared what Mary had told him the night before. There was no message for me about my mom, so I was a little disappointed. Then, we attended the English Mass at 10:00 a.m.

Peace is the central theme in Medjugorje, and we felt it all of the time. People were patient and kind. Our days were hot, but cool breezes blew often. Duke began calling them "Mary's breezes." The faith of the local people and pilgrims was incredible and inspiring.

Duke is resting in front of St. James' church with his favorite statue of Our Blessed Mother in the background.

After lunch we visited the Comunita' Cenacolo for young men with addictions, which was founded by a dynamic, tiny nun, named Mother Elvira Petrozzi. The men spend their days working and praying. They build everything themselves, including their housing. The community is supported by their crafts, gardening, and donations. They have no doctor or psychiatrist on staff; they rely only on God. They commit to staying there for three to five years, and their success rate for recovery from their addictions is 90 percent! Mother Elvira has opened seventy-one houses in twenty countries over the past twenty-five years.

After this visit, Duke and I meandered around Medjugorje separately and prayed privately. I spotted the same young man I had seen the day before. I don't want to give the impression that I was stalking him, but I was drawn to him, and I admit I followed him down a path once and took his picture from a distance.

About 5:30 p.m. Duke and I were outside the church saying our rosary, when he left to go to the restroom and smoke a cigarette. He said he heard a woman's voice behind him pleading, "Don't put that poison in your body." He turned around and saw no one, and then knew that it was our Blessed Mother asking him, lovingly, to stop smoking. She told him that his migraines were caused by his smoking, and that she would ask her Son to help him stop smoking and cure his headaches. Duke threw away his cigarettes immediately and didn't have an urge to smoke again - until we were at the airport in Zurich on the way home! We have never been saints and we have our weaknesses! So, unfortunately, his smoking and headaches continued for many years.

At 6:00 p.m. that Tuesday, I went to the side of church where confessions were being held. There were about fifteen to twenty lines; each designated for a specific language. As I stood in the long English-speaking line, I noticed a familiar voice behind me whisper, "I hear he's really mean." I turned around, and there was Father Bill. He was teasing me, because the priest hearing my confession was probably in his eighties, from Ireland, and very gentle and kind.

As soon as I stepped into the confessional room, about the size of a closet, I felt that I was in the presence of God the Father. After the priest had given me his blessing, he pushed a Miraculous Medal toward me across the kneeler. He said, "I had this with me on Apparition Hill last night, and

Mary blessed it. I have blessed it also." I held it in my hand like it was the most precious gem in the world. Then he slid two more towards me and said casually, "Oh, have two more!"

I walked out of that confessional on cloud nine! I put one medal on my necklace chain right away, gave another one to Duke as soon as we met, and I put the third in the yellow plastic bag I was using to collect all of my sacramentals. After each Mass I would hold up my bag to have the items blessed.

It's a funny thing; I am not a shopper and had no intention of buying anything to take home with me, but I could not pass a gift shop without stopping in. I ended up buying several rosaries, medals, and other holy objects. Duke bought three copies of the same portrait of Jesus praying. We compared purchases each evening, and discovered that neither of us knew to whom we would give each object, but we trusted that the Holy Spirit would let us know eventually. As we discovered in a VHS tape we brought home, Ivan had the same portrait of Jesus that Duke had purchased. It was hanging on the wall in his home where he had his private apparitions. We surmised that Our Blessed Mother liked that portrait of Jesus as much as Duke did.

After confession, I went to the church to find Duke and to finish the rosary. Then we stayed for the Croatian Mass. Medjugorje is as close as it comes to heaven on earth. There were countless voices in many languages singing and praying together. Some of the songs in Latin we all knew. "Adeste Fideles" was wonderful and gave me goose bumps, when people from all nationalities sang it together.

After Mass, there was a healing service. I remember feeling unusually healthy the entire time I was in this holy village, even though we went without food for long periods of time, and we were walking or climbing on rocks often. I didn't even miss things, like chocolate or hamburgers, that I would normally crave.

We had dinner about 9:00 p.m. that night. We were all very tired, as we talked about our day. I quietly encouraged Duke to share Our Lady's message, but he said he was not ready yet. After the general conversation died, we went straight to bed. It was a wonderful, miraculous day! My heart was filled with joy, as Duke and I were growing closer and closer to our Lady.

On Wednesday, after morning prayers and breakfast, we left at 7:00 a.m. to climb Apparition Hill. I had continued to fast on bread and water on Wednesdays and Fridays, so I packed a piece of bread for my lunch after eating a piece for breakfast.

The villagers had erected bas-relief statues on the hill to represent the mysteries of the rosary. Father Bill led us in prayer as we climbed. We said the joyful mysteries on the way up to the sight of the first apparition on June 24, 1981. We said the sorrowful mysteries as we circled the top of the hill, and we said the glorious mysteries as we descended the hill. I thanked Jesus often, throughout the trip, for my health and ability to keep up with the strenuous schedule.

At 9:00 a.m. we heard Jakov, the youngest visionary, speak outside of his home. He told us about his visits to heaven and hell. He said that heaven was "too wonderful to imagine and that hell was too awful to imagine." He asked us to pray for peace in our hearts and in our families. He also encouraged family prayer and fasting. He reminded us, "Today is Wednesday, a fasting day."

At 10:00 a.m. we went to the English Mass and then we heard Father Svet, a parish priest, speak in the Pilgrim's Hall. He said that we were all called to make this pilgrimage, and that none of us came by accident. That was also the first time we saw the painting of Mary based on the six visionaries' descriptions. They said that this was the closest likeness to her, but that it doesn't compare to her beauty.

Duke is looking at Mary's painting for the first time.

Then, Duke and I decided to pray separately until meeting again at 5:00 p.m. for rosary and Mass at the church. I decided to go back up Apparition Hill alone. I knew that my dad was scheduled for surgery that day, and I wanted to be on the hill while he was under the knife. As I prayed the third joyful mystery, the birth of Jesus, a blue butterfly stayed close to me, and followed me throughout my climb. As I prayed the third sorrowful mystery I meditated on the crowning of thorns. I backed up a bit to see the bas-relief better, as the shadows were hiding some of the details of the etching. I wasn't looking behind me and I backed into a thorn tree that pierced my scalp. I jerked away from the pain. You can imagine how my meditation rose to a whole new level! At the marker indicating the sight of Mary's first apparition, I prayed for my dad, and sat on a rock and ate my bread and water.

After returning from the hill, I went to the front of St. James' Church to meet Duke at 5:00 p.m. as planned. He was already there, sitting on a low brick wall that encircled the raised flower beds. He was surrounded by butterflies and had a silly grin on his face. They were flying around his head, sitting on his shoulders and fluttering in front of his face. He asked me, "Do you want to know why these butterflies are here?" I watched them for a while. Duke made no attempt to shoo them away. "Sure, I do," I responded. "Well", he said, "Mary is not happy with me for not sharing her message at dinner last night, so she sent these butterflies to encourage me to tell them all about it tonight." I said, "Well, why didn't she send a swarm of bees?" He just grinned his silly grin and said, "That's not her style." I remember thinking, "How does he know her style already?" But he did, probably from the first conversation they had on July third.

Before dinner that night, Father Bill told us that we would be leaving the house at 5:00 a.m. the next morning to climb Cross Mountain, otherwise known as Mt. Krizevac. He said it was an arduous trek, twice as hard as the climb up Apparition Hill. He said that we would not get our breakfast until after we returned back to the house. As I contemplated my evening and morning, I decided to end my fast and eat whatever was served for dinner that night. I reasoned that since I had only eaten two pieces of bread all day, and wouldn't have another chance to eat again until after climbing the mountain the next day, I'd better fortify my body with good food at dinner and get a good night's sleep.

After dinner, I encouraged Duke to share the message he had received from Mary on Tuesday, but he was still afraid. He was sure no one would believe him, and they would ridicule him. He was extremely shy about talking to others, regardless of the topic. Duke told me once, that he took an "F" in a speech class in high school rather than make the required speech. He was especially intimidated by all of the devout Catholics in our group, which included Father Bill.

Thursday morning, at first light, we began our assent of Cross Mountain. The story goes that in 1933, the villagers built a concrete cross on top of this mountain to commemorate the one thousand, nine hundredth year anniversary of Jesus' death. Some claim that there is a piece of the true cross enclosed within. Building the cross was not an easy job. There weren't any trails up the mountain back then. The village was suffering from an economic depression at that time, as was most of the world. People had to carry all of the equipment and materials up the hill, mix the concrete at the top, and form the cross. It is perhaps one of the reasons Mary chose this small parish to visit in 1981. Another bit of interesting history about the parish is that in 1966, the parish priest rebuilt St. James Church large enough to hold two thousand parishioners. Everyone questioned why he would build such a large church when there were only about three hundred families in the community at that time. Only a couple of weeks after the apparitions began, the church was filled to capacity each day. Eventually, they had to add loud speakers to the outside of the building so the over-flow crowd could participate in Mass. Then, they had to build an out-door area in the back of church to accommodate crowds of ten thousand people or more.

The climb up Cross Mountain took us one and a half hours to arrive at the top. We stopped along the way to say the "Stations of the Cross." We arrived near the top and found a marker where Father Slavko Barbaric had died in November, 2000. He had been a spiritual advisor for the visionaries prior to his death.

Our guide spoke very highly of him, and we were fascinated by her stories of Father Slavko.

She said he would climb Cross Mountain and Apparition Hill each day with a trash bag to clean up the litter pilgrims left. He spoke five languages fluently, and was learning Korean when he died. He wanted to minister to all pilgrims who came to this holy place, in their own language. I suggest to you, the reader, to research more about this remarkable priest.

This station is where people left flowers in memory of Father Slavko.

When we reached the top, I was surprised to find butterflies hovering and landing on the rocks near my feet. They were plain, colorless rocks with no flowers nearby. I took several pictures of the rocks, and when I had the film developed, no butterflies appeared.

Our guide suggested that we lay our burdens down at the foot of the cross, and give them to Jesus. We did this separately and in silence.

As our group was assembling for the climb down the mountain, I glanced once more at the cross, and saw the same young man I had found at the Risen Jesus statue. I whispered to Duke that this was the same pious young man I had been seeing around the village. Duke said he had also noticed that boy. I felt a need to meet him. As I approached the young man I said, "May I hug you? You are so good." He just stood under the cross, held out his arms and said, "I love you." I looked into the most beautiful brown eyes I had ever seen, and put my arms around him. We held each other for a minute or so, as I cried tears of joy and felt the unfathomable love of Jesus. I cried the rest of the way down the mountain.

At the bottom, we waited in an outdoor café for the rest of our group to descend. I saw "my boy", as I was referring to him by then, come down bare footed, grab his sandals at the bottom of the hill, and walk to his group waiting near our table. I gave him a shy wave, to indicate that we had just had a special moment at the top of the mountain. He didn't wave back. He passed right by and joined his group, all speaking Italian. God gave me my own miracle through this devout young man. Jesus spoke to me through him, and I don't think the boy was even aware of the way God had used him.

Father Bill was a little concerned about me, because I was still crying as we got into the cab to return to our boarding house. He asked me what had happened. All I could say was that I had hugged Jesus at the top of the mountain, and He told me that He loved me. Duke assured Father Bill that I was fine. He knew that I tended to cry when I was touched by God. I sometimes cry after receiving the Holy Eucharist, so this was nothing new for my husband.

Our group arrived back to the house around 9:00 a.m. for breakfast. As we ate, we shared our experiences. One man in our group, who had impressed me as being very devout, said that as we were at the Fourth Station of the Cross, when Jesus meets his Mother, he heard Mary's voice speaking to him. Part of the reading at the Station was, "Who will comfort her?" Mary told him, "You will comfort me."

After breakfast we walked to St. James Church for the English Mass. Before Mass began, I went up to my favorite statue of Mary, just to the right of the altar. As I looked into her eyes, they came alive. She looked at me with eyes of love and disappointment. Then, the message came to me internally, "Don't you think My Son could have helped you up that mountain without your dinner last night? You could have kept your fast yesterday, and still have been strong enough for the climb."

I was so ashamed that I started crying all over again! This time because I had disappointed my loving Mother.

At dinner that night, I encouraged Duke to share the message he had been given for "all who will listen." Again, he could not bring himself to tell anyone about it. After dinner, about four women and I decided to take a walk. One of the women told us that she had lost her daughter to cancer when she was only twenty-one years old. She said, "Now I have a daughter in heaven, and I pray for her intercession all of the time." A very clear thought came to me and I announced joyfully, "I have a daughter in heaven, too, and her name is Mary Ann." Many years earlier, I had lost a child before I knew I was pregnant. I remember a sharp pain and a lot of bleeding. I went to a doctor and he told me I had experienced a "spontaneous abortion." I was saddened at first, but never really thought about it after that, until that evening in Medjugorje. Since then, I have asked Mary Ann to intercede often for members of my family.

Friday, July 13, was a fasting day again. I was DETERMINED to fast on only bread and water until breakfast Saturday! I didn't want to disappoint my Blessed Mother again, no matter what physical challenges we might face. I am sure that Jesus helped me with my fast, because I didn't feel tired all day. Duke had decided to fast on bread and water as well. This was his first experience with this type of fast.

I decided to climb Cross Mountain by myself after the 10:00 a.m. Holy Mass. Again, I had packed a slice of bread and a bottle of water to eat on the top of the mountain. As I sat under the cross to eat, I noticed a man sitting there quietly. He had walked up the mountain without his shoes. We often saw pairs of shoes at the bottom of Cross Mountain, as well as Apparition Hill, left by people who chose to do that particular penance. I offered him half of my bread and some water. He said, "No, thank you," with a beautiful smile. He told me that each Friday he climbs Cross Mountain and meditates on Jesus' passion. He fasts from all food and drink, including water, until 3:00 p.m. I remember finding a half-eaten apple on the top of the hill. I began thinking that I could clean it off and get at least something else to eat besides the piece of bread. But I remembered Mary's eyes of disappointment on Thursday morning, and I reaffirmed my decision to fast until breakfast Saturday morning.

Duke told me that he had had several personal conversations with Mary while I was on the mountain. He asked her for a sign to prove that he was not imagining all of what he had been experiencing. She told him to look at the sun. He did, and saw the sun turn blue and pulsate and shoot a beam of light to the ground. Then she said, "Now will you do as I ask?" and he said, "Yes, Mother." However, at dinner that night, he got nervous and couldn't bring himself to share what had been happening to him.

As we had been fasting all day, we had trouble getting to sleep that night. At midnight, Duke got up, got dressed and went out on a quest for a hamburger. He returned about an hour later declaring that he had found something to eat, but it was probably a donkey-burger. We had a good laugh over that.

Our last full day in this holy place arrived all too soon. It was Saturday, July 14, our twenty-eighth wedding anniversary. I woke up at 5:45 a.m. feeling great. Not one muscle hurt, and I did not have a headache, which was typical when fasting on bread and water. I was SOOO looking forward to breakfast. I wrote in my journal, "I hope we have eggs."

After breakfast we attended the 10:00 a.m. Mass. Father Bill was the main celebrant for the Mass and I had been asked to take the first reading. I remember his homily focused on Matthew 9:37 **"The harvest is abundant but the laborers are few."** He encouraged us all to be laborers in God's vineyards when we returned home.

Our group then met for lunch near the church. After lunch we took a bus ride to Father Jozo Zovko's church. (He is the priest portrayed by Martin Sheen in the movie, Gospa.) We went into a chapel with a life-sized Jesus hanging on the cross, with real hair and toenails. We also saw the statue of "Our Lady of Grace" that has taken on life-like qualities from time to time.

After we arrived back to the village of Medjugorje, I went off to pray privately and Duke went to the local cemetery to find Father Slavko's grave. He said he was drawn to that priest, but he didn't understand why. Later, Mary told him that he should pray to Father Slavko Barbaric for intercessory help; that he would become his "special" Saint. We discovered a few days after we got home that July 14 was the anniversary of Father Slavko's ordination. What a God-incidence!

About 5:45 p.m. I saw "my boy" walk into the church for the 6:00 p.m. Croatian Mass. He stayed very devout, kneeling on the floor, as he had given up his pew for someone else. When we all stood, he was like a child trying to see a parade, bouncing on his tip-toes to see everything. He seemed so excited to be there. During communion, we faced each other, but he did not show any sign of recognition. He still had no idea he had become Jesus for me during that moment on the mountain top!

Dinner that night was memorable. Duke finally shared all that had been happening to him, and he read the message that our Blessed Mother had given him Tuesday morning. No one called him a liar or crazy. Father Bill leaned across the table and asked Duke, "What does her voice sound like?" Duke said, "It is hard to describe. It is so sweet, full of love, and almost musical."

We celebrated our twenty-eighth wedding anniversary with a special heart-shaped cake and simple presents. It was the best anniversary we ever had!

At 1:30 a.m., on Sunday, July 15, many members of our group squeezed into in Father Bill's room for Mass. It was the only opportunity for us to make our Sunday obligation, as that was our travel day, and our driver was due to arrive at 2:30 a.m. to take us to the airport. Before we parted ways, Father Bill warned all of us that Satan would do whatever he could to disturb our peace. He advised us to pray for St. Michael's protection as we traveled home. That was great advice, because Satan began to target us in many ways. The evil one was determined to ruin our peace and joy.

5

Back Home Again

We arrived home Sunday evening about 10:30 p.m. I unpacked only a few items before going to bed. I had purchased many things I had not planned to buy, because each time I walked past a gift shop, I would get a "nudge" to go in and buy a rosary, a holy medal, or a crucifix.

I had also brought special rosaries with me that friends had given me before we left for Medjugorje, to have blessed while there. One was a friend's mother's first communion rosary from about 1930. Father Bill had blessed all of these items during our last dinner on Saturday night. Mary had also blessed them during her visit on Apparition Hill. I carefully took them out of my backpack and laid them on the kitchen table. All of the blessed sacramentals I had bought, and all that I had taken with me, were in a yellow plastic bag.

Monday morning, I called the hospital where Dad had his surgery and found out that he was permitted to go home. I told the nurse I would come by and pick him up that morning. I went to 8:30 a.m. mass and then to the hospital. I stayed with him at his condo, making sure he was settled in until about 3:00 p.m., and then drove home.

The first thing I wanted to do was sort through the rosaries and medals and decide what to do with them. I knew that the Holy Spirit would guide me in those decisions.

I couldn't find the yellow plastic bag anywhere. I asked my daughter, who was living with us at the time, where it was, and she said she hadn't seen it. Duke was visiting his mother in Indiana, so when he got home, I asked him where my bag was. He said he didn't know what I was talking about. I began to panic. I described the bag again, and exactly where I had left it. Duke went into the garage and came back carrying THE BAG. He said he had decided to clean up while I was busy visiting my dad, thought it was trash and threw it into the garbage can. Three days later, I couldn't find the bag again, and finally found it under the chair cushion in our bedroom. The evil one certainly didn't want people to have those sacramentals!

After we returned, Mary continued to tell Duke what she wanted us to do. She continued to give him messages to share, and he continued to wonder, "why me?"

The reactions of our family members were varied. Some did not believe us. That hurt, but we didn't spend a lot of energy trying to prove it was real. We just let time go by, and hoped that seeing our lives change might be proof enough. Sometimes, even Duke and I had doubts that it was all real, and then Mary would give Duke a message or something would happen, to prove to us that it was really happening.

One of the first things we did was to invite our friends from church, work, and Marriage Encounter to our home on July 21 to hear our stories. We were (at least I was) bursting to share what we had experienced in the village of Mary's apparitions. I had placed books, VHS tapes, magazines, photos and other bits of information about Medjugorje on our dining room table as a supplement to our talk. We encouraged people to borrow what they wanted, and to return the materials when they finished with them.

Before anyone came, I was overcome with joy and emotion, knowing that we were doing God's will. It was very hard for Duke; he was nervous.

We presented to about forty people that first time; many of whom I didn't know, because friends had invited friends. We talked for two and a half hours before I realized that we should stop and let folks get up and walk around, get a refreshment, and then ask questions. I remember one person asking Duke about the rosary. "Isn't it tiresome and boring to be saying the same prayers over and over?" Duke's reply was unforgettable. "Not for me. Each prayer is like a diamond I am offering to Our Lady. Each prayer is special and unique."

Another thing we did was to find a spiritual advisor. Father Bill had recommended that to us before we left, as did one other person. The third person to give us that recommendation was Mother Angelica, during one of her live broadcasts on EWTN. Duke and I were watching the program together and she looked straight at the camera (and us), pointed her finger at us and said, "You need to find a spiritual advisor." We looked at each other and laughed. We had gotten the message loud and clear.

So, I contacted Father Ray Favret, a retired priest assigned to help our parish of St. John the Evangelist in West Chester, Ohio. I knew he had been to Medjugorje and was devoted to Our Blessed Mother. I thought he would be the best person for us to talk to. I made an appointment to meet with him on a Saturday afternoon. We sat in the parking lot for about fifteen minutes before I could get Duke out of the car. He was so worried that Father Ray would reject his claims and call him a liar, a dreamer, or a crazy person. We had five messages from Our Blessed Mother by this time, so we brought them for Father to read.

These are the messages from Our Blessed Mother (plus the message from July 10) that we brought to Father Ray on Saturday, August 27, 2001:

Tuesday, 8/7/2001

"My Angel,

Praise be to Jesus! As always, I send you my motherly love. I can see that my love has taken hold in your heart. When I look upon you now, I see my love being reflected back as your love for me! It is such a blessing to me!

You have been questioning about the Holy Spirit.[1] I will try to explain in a manner which you can understand. The Holy Spirit is the Breath of God. It is God's Essence. God the Father sends the Holy Spirit into the world to do His Will. The Holy Spirit spoke to Moses from the burning bush, He spoke to the prophets, He inspired the Holy Scriptures and today He speaks to men's hearts urging them to conversion. The Holy Spirit is omnipotent and omnipresent. Do not pray for the Holy Spirit to come into your heart lightly. It is a powerful prayer, if you are praying from the heart. So many call on the Holy Spirit, but it is just words. My children, take special care not to take the name of the Holy Spirit in vain, for this is an unpardonable sin!

Many people do not pray because they say that they do not know what to say. Did not my Son give them the Lord's prayer, which is a very powerful prayer? Also, you have the Rosary which is the most blessed of prayers. Every "Hail Mary" that you pray from the heart is a special gift of love to me. Every time you meditate on one of the mysteries, it is a special gift for my Son and I, but I tell you, my angel, very few stop to meditate on what God the Father's heart was experiencing at this time, especially the sorrowful mysteries. You will never know the complete and utter anguish that the Father felt. It was only His love and mercy for each and every one of you that stayed God's hand from sending a legion of angels to rescue His Son from His suffering!

Whenever you pray, always pray from your heart. Prayer that is not from the heart is just so much noise! Prayer is merely conversation between your heart and the Lord's heart. You can talk for hours to your friends. You tell them everything, but you cannot do the same with my Son? Open your hearts to Him, and I tell you the truth, He will surely be with you always!

My angel, tell this message to all who will listen."
Duke then said, "I love you mother."
And She responded, "I love you too. Thank you, my Angel, for having responded to my call."

> **"O Lord, you have searched me and you know me. You know when I sit and when I rise; you perceive my thoughts from afar. You discern my going out and my lying down; you are familiar with all of my ways. Before a word is on my tongue you know it completely; O Lord."**
> **Psalm 139: 1-4**

8/15/2001 – Feast of the Assumption

"My Angel[2],

I send you my motherly love and blessings. It gave me great joy watching you pray together last night. Thank you for your devotion. Seeing families praying together always brings tears of joy to my eyes.

You are blessed, my angel, for the Holy Spirit has impressed upon your heart that this is the time of the final harvest. Now, my children, I need you to help me bring all souls to my Son. You should rejoice and be glad for the hour of your deliverance is at hand. So long I have interceded on your behalf to the Father, bringing before Him your prayers and your fasting in order to obtain more time for your conversion. The Father has said to me, 'Mary, can you not see how the just are suffering with the unjust? I cannot abide their iniquity any longer. It is time.' God's plan is already being carried out.

When I leave my sign in the Holy Places, the world will have seven days plus one day of Grace to make their final decision as to whom they will serve. The Holy Spirit will be poured out upon the world as it never has been before! God will grant mankind a special Grace. You will see your soul as God the Father sees your soul. You will know beyond any doubt where you are spiritually.

Please do not wait to consecrate your heart to my Son. Surrender your will to Him! Soon the world will enter a time of darkness and tribulation. If you belong to my Son, He will claim you as His own and not one hair of your head will be harmed.

Be like John crying in the wilderness, for I tell you the truth, my Son is coming soon!

Courage, my angel, and remember that I will be with you always. Go in peace to love and serve the Lord. Thank you for responding to my call."

8/20/2001

"My Angel,

I send you my motherly love and blessings. Your love for me continues to grow in abundance. It causes my heart to leap for joy! Thank you for your devotion. Continue to say the rosary each day with Claire. Continue to pray from your heart. I was so touched that you miss your Mother[3]. That is why I am coming to you today.

I wish to speak to you today, my angel, about marriage and families. Too many couples fail to recognize that marriage is a sacrament. It is a

Holy Covenant between God and the couple. They fail to include the Father as part of their union.

I pour out my motherly love and blessings upon the Marriage Encounter movement. So much has been accomplished by their efforts. The fruits of their efforts are expanding in ways that they cannot imagine; but, my angel, they need to put even more emphasis on God's role in the marriage and the responsibility that they have in regards to the children.

From marriage comes the children. Every child is a gift from the Father. Be kind, gentle and patient with your children. Pray for those that practice the hideous sin of abortion. I tell you the truth, my angel, it would have been better for them if they had never been born.

Bring up your children in Godliness. Tell them Bible stories, pray with them, and take them to Holy Mass. I tell you the truth, my angel, you will be held accountable to the Father for your children!

The families that pray together, and that have consecrated their hearts to my Son, are changing the world. Of that you can be certain. Praise, Jesus!

I must go now, my Angel, but I will come again. I love you more than you can ever know. Tell all that will listen and pray, pray, pray for those who will not. Thank you for responding to my call."

8/25/2001

"My Angel,

I send you my Motherly love and blessings!

When my Son gave His life for the salvation of mankind, a new covenant was formed between God, the Father, and His children. At the heart of this new covenant is the Lord's Day. The Father intended for this day to be a special day of communion between mankind and God.

Most of my children leave Holy Mass and go about their daily lives as if the Lord's Day was just any other day. The Lord's Day should be kept Holy! Put aside your daily cares and chores and meditate on the Father, the Son, and the Holy Spirit. Spend this time praying from your hearts and studying the Holy Scriptures. It is my heart's deepest desire to lead all my children to greater holiness.

My angel, you must tell my children. They do not know! Tell all who will listen, my dearest one. Go in peace to love and serve the Lord. Thank you for responding to my call."

I remember Father Ray Favret believing all that Duke told him, asking him questions, and then reading the messages. As he read the messages, his comments included, "Wow, people really need to hear this!" His main advice to us at that time was to share the messages one at a time, so that people would not be overwhelmed. Duke was very relieved and encouraged after our meeting with Father Ray.[4]

One of my favorite memories of those early days is of a lady named Amy. Amy was invited to our house the night of our first presentation by one of my CRHP sisters. I had never met her.

When I was telling the story of my confession to the Irish Priest, I mentioned that the third Miraculous Medal he had given me was upstairs in my bedroom, and that I was waiting for the Holy Spirit to tell me who should receive it.

A week later, I was ironing in my kitchen, and my doorbell rang. It was Amy returning a book she had borrowed the Saturday before. As she stood on my porch, I invited her into my kitchen to see our rose bush in the back yard. Duke had planted two Peace Roses a few years earlier; one on each side of a trellis. In the middle of the trellis was a two-foot statue of Our Lady of Grace. In the week since our presentation, two branches, one from each side of the trellis, had grown across the back of Mary's head. I remember taking this as a sign that Mary was pleased with our presentation.

I was very excited to show the new growth of the rose bushes to Amy. She was reluctant to come in, saying she was returning from the gym and was sweaty. I told her I was ironing and didn't care. As she looked at the rose bushes through my kitchen window, a thought came to me to give her one of the rosaries I had bought in Medjugorje. But, before I could run upstairs to get it, Amy took a rosary out of her pocket to show me. She had bought it since the Saturday before, and had learned to say the prayers. It was a small rosary made of clear purple stones. Amy explained to me that she wasn't Catholic, but loved our story and wanted to learn more about the rosary and Our Blessed Mother. So, I told her to wait a minute while I ran upstairs. As I went through my bag of "gifts", I decided to give her the third miraculous medal the priest had given to me in the confessional. I came down the stairs and said, "I think the Holy Spirit wants you to have this." She immediately closed her fist and said, "No, I'm not worthy, I'm not worthy." Amy started to leave and I insisted she take it. I had to pry her fingers loose, so I could put the medal in her palm. She began to cry and left.

Amy returned many times to our rosary prayer group, and we got to know each other well. I found out over time, that when I had said during my presentation, "The Holy Spirit will tell me who should get the Miraculous Medal," Amy heard a voice tell her, "It's for you." When she went home to her husband that evening, she told him all that we had shared, and what God had said to her. Her husband told her she was nuts. He told her that she wasn't a Catholic, she wasn't my friend, and would probably never see me again. When Amy went home the next Saturday, opened her hand, and showed her husband the medal, he was blown away! I love the way the Holy Spirit works through us when we are open to His promptings.

The third thing we did, after returning home, was to initiate a rosary group in our home on Tuesday and Thursday evenings at 7:00 p.m. It was not formal. All friends, co-workers and family members were invited without RSVPs, and there was no commitment to come every time. About the fourth time this group met, I put one of the blessed medals I had purchased in Medjugorje on a coffee table, and decided that the first person the Holy Spirit directed to come into our home that night would get the medal. It was a particularly beautiful medal of Our Lady in blue. A woman from my CRHP group, named Vi, came in first. She was in her late seventies, and very devout. When I told her that she was selected to get the medal, she cried tears of joy. Her daughter told me, at Vi's funeral, that she never took it off, even for showers, so they buried her in it.

There were many times in the first few months after our return, that the evil one put thoughts into our minds to discredit the messages and our experiences. When I would begin to doubt what was happening, Mary would often give Duke a personal message for someone, to reassure both of us that what was happening was real.

One time Our Blessed Mother gave Duke a message to "give to my daughter." It was a message about someone named Eric. Duke told me that he was sure it was for a particular lady who came regularly to our rosary group. I asked him how he could be sure, and he couldn't explain; he just knew. So, we asked that lady privately if she knew anyone named Eric. She said that Eric was her son, so Duke gave her the message. She read it privately and it touched her deeply. I imagine she still has the message.

Another time Duke said that Our Blessed Mother told him that my mother was in heaven, but had spent "some time" in purgatory[5]. The reason for this was because at her final confession, she deliberately withheld a sin. Then he said that he had been given a glimpse of my mom in heaven. He said, "She is so beautiful! She has shoulder-length, very thick, wavy hair." Duke had never known my mom before she suffered from Lupus. She had been physically affected by pain and medication since 1970. I said, "How do you know it was my mom? She was never beautiful when you knew her, and she always had thin, straight hair; although it was always mom's wish to have beautiful wavy hair." He said, "I just know. She is very happy." He then gave me a personal message from my mom that contained things he could never have known, including the nickname mom had given me when I was very young.

Another thing I realized early on, was that the messages Duke was given contained words that were not part of his vocabulary. The phrasing wasn't his. When I read them carefully, it was not something Duke could have created on his own.

The other thing that convinced me that everything Duke said was true, was his fear and reluctance to bring attention to himself. He was very embarrassed to be the one to say, "This is happening to me." He would have done anything to avoid the attention, but he did not want to disobey or disappoint his heavenly Mother. He loved her so much from the very first time she spoke to him. Sometimes, with sensitive messages, he was even more reluctant to share them. He would tell me not to type it or share with others for a week or more.

We did have physical evidence that God was touching our lives in a special way. Before we left for Medjugorje, I decided to take a rosary with me that my mom had given me in 1974. It had clear blue glass beads and silver-colored links and crucifix. Duke took the rosary he had been given by our church when he was confirmed, which also had silver links. I had read about rosaries turning gold in Medjugorje, so I showed both of my children my silver links and crucifix before we left, and said, "Maybe when I come back, it will all have turned to a golden color!" Our rosaries did not change color in Medjugorje.

However, when we got back, I noticed that the link that connected the crucifix to the rest of the rosary had turned golden. A week later, I noticed that the three larger links that connect the central medal to each of the three strands of the rosary had turned golden. A week later, I noticed that each of the small links that connected each "Hail Mary" bead had turned golden. Duke and I compared rosaries and they had both changed in the same way. Mary told him that the changes in our rosaries was her gift to us. She said that if the links connecting the "Our Fathers" ever turned golden, that would be a gift from Jesus. So, of course, these became our favorite rosaries. And, like little children, we would check often for our gift from Jesus. Years went by and we saw no changes in the rosaries.

One evening, during the sorrowful mysteries, Duke silently told Jesus that he wanted to help Him carry His cross. Soon after this offer, he began to develop severe shoulder pain. It hurt him so badly, that he went to a doctor. The doctor couldn't locate the source of Duke's pain, but gave him cortisone shots in his shoulder for about six months.

We were also attacked by evil spirits, especially before presentations. The first time was the night before we were scheduled to speak to a group at Good Shepherd church. Duke said he woke up suddenly when a slimy, smelly hand was placed over his nose and mouth. A creepy voice said, "Don't mess with me, maggot. You don't know who you are dealing with." Then the presence was gone. Duke woke me up and told me what had just happened to him. He was terrified. He wanted me to call Father Ray and ask him to come over to bless our house right away. It was 2:30 a.m.! There was no way I was going to call that dear old priest in the middle of the night. I told Duke that I had some holy water in the closet down the hall. He asked me to get it. I was afraid to move and told him to get it. Finally, I got up and started sprinkling Holy Water all over the house, and especially in our bedroom. After that, I always kept the holy water on my night stand.

Another night, I heard a crash, and found Duke in a fetal position on the floor of our bathroom. He said an evil spirit had picked him up and thrown him across the room. We just prayed a lot for Mary and God's help when those things occurred. They weren't frequent, fortunately.

We also realized that Satan was trying to break up our marriage. I remember one specific time when every little thing Duke did, bothered me. I had thoughts of how nice life would be without him. After two days of this, we were saying our rosary together, and I told Duke what kind of thoughts I had been having. He confessed to me that he had been experiencing the same thoughts. We agreed that we needed to be extra vigilant with our prayers and our kindness toward one another. We became determined not to let Satan have his way. But we were human and sinful, and it was not always easy.

During the Good Friday service of 2002, Duke had a remarkable experience. As we were adoring the cross, he was transported to the site of Jesus' crucifixion. After we got home, he asked me to smell his hands. I smelled something different, but couldn't place it. He told me the smell was from the spices the women were using to prepare Jesus' body for the grave. He told me he had helped to take Jesus' body off of the cross. He then had the job of supplying fresh water from the well for the women who were washing Jesus' body. Duke wept as he told me how quickly the bowls of water turned red. He said he had to go back to the well over and over again, because there was so much blood. It was several days before the smell left his hands.

That experience at the foot of the cross was his first "glimpse," as he called those experiences. There were many others throughout the years. Often, he would be given a glimpse during our rosary as we meditated on a mystery. Mary instructed our prayer group, through Duke, that when he appeared to be talking to her, or having a glimpse, we should continue our rosary until the end. We were aware that something was happening when Duke would stop praying out loud, and change his demeaner. Sometimes he would kneel and hold both arms out, while holding onto the crucifix of the rosary. Sometimes we would see his lips move, and not hear him speaking. We were obedient, however, and continued praying until we finished our mysteries.

After the rosary, we were all very anxious to find out what had happened. Sometimes it was very simple. He would tell us that Mary had appeared and smiled at us and blessed us. Often, he could not tell us right away what had happened. He would just need to be silent and pray alone. There was not a schedule for her visits or the glimpses, so we could rarely anticipate an event.

Duke continued to see the miracle of the sun[6] after we returned home from Medjugorje. This occurred perhaps four times a year until about 2006. Usually he would describe it as a colorful, spinning ball. Sometimes we would be driving, or sitting on our back deck, and he would get excited and tell me to look at the sun. I explained to him that I would burn my retina if I tried, and he had a hard time believing that I could not see it.

Once, as we got closer to July 2002, Mary told Duke that she would visit us in our home during our regular rosary group on "their anniversary." Duke got a kick out of her reference to their anniversary. So, July 3 became a special date for us. It also happens to be the feast day of St. Thomas, the doubter. Our Blessed Mother has a wonderful sense of humor!

She told Duke to buy as many miraculous medals as he could for that night. She said that she would bless them when she came, and that we should distribute them to all who came. Duke went to two religious stores and bought all of the medals they had. We filled a big bowl with them in the middle of our family room. Our house was packed and we had a wonderful "anniversary party." She blessed the medals and all who were present received at least one.

I know of one miraculous cure that occurred related to one of those medals. The son of one of the attendees was scheduled for surgery. His mom pinned the medal to his hospital gown, and when they did another test to prepare for the surgery, they could no longer find the defect in his heart, and cancelled the surgery.

Toward the end of 2002, Mary told Duke to find Father Leroy Smith at Our Lady of the Holy Spirit Center in Norwood. I had not been there since that wonderful night of August 31, 1999, and Duke had never been there. I did not know what Father Smith looked like.

When we parked and got out of the car, Duke said, "This feels like I'm back in Medjugorje. I can feel her presence." We walked into the building and didn't see anyone until we found a guy wearing white painter's overalls, up on a scaffold, smoking a cigarette, and working on a mosaic at the end of one hallway.

The man said, "Can I help you?" in a deep voice. Duke said, "We're looking for Father Smith." The man said, "You've found him." He climbed down, and we told him we were there because Our Lady told us to find him. He took us into an office and we talked to him for at least an hour. Duke did most of the talking, which was unusual. When he told Father Smith about how the butterflies had fluttered around his head, Father Smith told us that butterflies can be a sign of Mary's presence. I had never heard that, but it was comforting and reassuring to know, especially since I had encountered butterflies in other ways. I think Duke felt very comfortable talking to Father Smith, which was not the norm for him. As the years went by, I would sometimes find Duke and Father Smith sitting on the garden steps at OLHSC, talking and smoking cigarettes together.

Father Smith invited Duke and I to speak about our experiences in Medjugorje to a group assembled at Our Lady of the Holy Spirit Center for Midnight Mass Dec. 31/Jan 1, 2003.

Soon after that, Father Smith assembled a panel consisting of three priests and Gerald Ross; all very knowledgeable regarding Marian apparitions.

They interviewed Duke several times and examined the messages he had received up to that time. After months of examination, they declared, "Calvin Patterson and his messages have been affirmed authentic and worthy of instruction." This notice was published in the August/September 2003 edition of the "Our Lady of the Holy Spirit Center Newsletter", volume 10 issue 5. They also published two messages Duke had been given by Mary for "all who will listen" in that edition. They continued to publish Mary's messages given through Duke for the next three editions.

As we came to know Father Smith and OLHSC, Duke began to volunteer there; first in the gardens, and then, when his back and knees deteriorated, in the library. He worked mostly with a lady named Sue, who was a wonderful daughter of Our Lady of Light.

After I retired in 2005, Duke and Sue convinced me to volunteer in the "Our Lady of Light" office. After a few months of volunteering, I had to find employment again, so I regretfully left my volunteer job. I really enjoyed getting to know Sue and others associated with the Our Lady of Light ministries. She was a very dynamic and loving lady. She has since passed away, and they named the library in her honor. Duke ended up volunteering there for five years before his health became too prohibitive. There is a plaque in the library, above the books about Mary, placed after his death, commemorating his work there.

In January 2003, I began a new job as the Human Resources Director for a large school district. During my first week on the job, I was sued for age, gender and disability discrimination. It was very worrisome for me. I got home rather late the day I got the notice of the lawsuit, and Duke met me at the door. He said, "What happened at work today?" Before I could answer he said that he had a message from Mary for me. He hadn't written it down as it was very simple. She said not to worry and to pray for the lady who was suing me. I knelt down immediately and prayed for her. I continued to pray for her for weeks. Finally, it was determined that the lawsuit had no grounds, and the problem melted away, as Mary had promised.

Another time I came home from work and Duke met me at the door and said, "What did you do?" Again, before I could answer, he said that Mary had a short message for me. "Go cleanse your soul." I honestly don't remember what sin I had committed, but I do remember that I went to confession right away.

Among the many things we were learning in the "School of Mary," was how much Our Blessed Mother loves us. She said once that "If you knew how much I loved you, you would cry tears of joy."

As any good mother, she is always near and wants the best for us, her children.

6

Our Rosary Group

Our rosary group began meeting as soon as we came home from Medjugorje in July 2001. We met for the first two years in our home, and then for a short time in Mary Ann's home. Finally, Our Blessed Mother requested that we meet in "My home"; that is, at Our Lady of the Holy Spirit Center in Norwood, Ohio. Since Duke had been volunteering there, it was an easy transition to make.

Finding a day of the week and a time to meet was not as easy, but eventually we met on Thursday evenings from 6:00 – 7:15. Sometimes we would attend Holy Mass at 7:15 after rosary. We continued meeting until 2015; two and a half years after Duke's death.

If the weather was nice, we would pray in front of the Our Lady of Lourdes' statue in one of the garden courtyards. If the weather was not amenable to outside prayer, we would meet on the right side of the Holy Rosary Chapel. After a few years, we moved our inside prayer location from the chapel to the library. Duke was volunteering in the library by then, and we had access to the space. The library contained at least fifteen statues of Our Blessed Mother, and sometimes we would, very carefully, take one off the shelf and put it on the table at the center of our prayer circle. Often, someone who had been visiting the Center would hear us praying and join us. We met some very interesting people that way.

When I decided to write this book, I asked some of our regular rosary group members to share a few of their favorite memories of those days. Here are some of the comments they gave me to include in this chapter:

From Amy:

"I came to your house as a "church going" non-believer. I prayed for years for God to give me a sign because I WANTED to believe soooooo badly, but it all sounded crazy to me. Well, He certainly answered my prayers. After hearing the words, "It's for you," (during your presentation in July 2001) I actually turned around to see if anyone may have just said that to me. I thought that I HAD to have imagined that, because you told us you had two children and certainly one of them would get the third medal. I was literally just finding my faith as I sat on that kitchen chair listening to your story. I thought there was no way that the special medal was for me because I wasn't even a believer! I wasn't worthy of such a precious gift. But God thought differently. Anyhow, I just thought that was an important part of the story because it shows how much God loves us even when we don't love or know Him. I truly can't stress enough that it's because you and Duke shared your story that I have the strong faith that I do now. I wish I could describe what happened inside of my heart that day. I was an instant Christian. I came to your house as a non-believer who wanted to believe so badly and who had prayed to God for YEARS to show me a "sign" and walked out 100 percent a believer. God certainly answered my prayers with you, Duke, and Beautiful Mary."

From Walt:

"One time, after rosary, Duke told each of us the name of his or her guardian angel. I had to run home quickly and research my name to see what it meant."

"One time, our rosary group met on Good Friday to climb the steps going up to Holy Cross-Immaculata Church in Cincinnati.[7] My wife was on her way up the hill when she glanced down and noticed that her rosary had turned golden, very suddenly, as she climbed and prayed. She shared this with me immediately and the rest of the group when we all reached the top of the steps."

From Mary Ann:

"When Mary would come into the room, (while we were praying the rosary) I could feel her. There was a general feeling of peace."

"I came to your first presentation after you returned from Medjugorje. I attempted to talk to Duke before you began speaking, but he was too nervous to talk. He was scared out of his mind!"

"One time we attended a talk at Amy's house. My husband came to hear the talk with me. When we walked out of her house to go home, we noticed a cloud in the shape of a heart. It was like a cookie-cutter heart, very sharp. There were no wispy edges to it."

"One time I gave my rosary to Duke to have it blessed by Mary. We were at my house, and after the rosary, he asked me for a piece of paper and a pen. He said Mary had given him a private message for me. He was writing so fast. I thought, 'He cannot be making this up; the words are just pouring out of him too fast.' Part of the message [from Mary] was, 'I kissed the crucifix out of love and reverence. My son kissed the crucifix because it is the symbol of His love for His brothers and sisters, His sacrifice, and His redemption of mankind.'"

From Joe:

"One time I wanted to have my rosaries blessed. Duke told me to put them in front of Mary's statue so she could bless them if she came that night. After our rosary, Duke told me that she did bless them, but in a most unusual way. Duke said she sang the blessing. He had never seen her do that before. I didn't tell anyone at the time, but I used to sing in our church choir. So, that was very special for me."

"One time, before we started praying, I overheard Duke talking about someone, who had been volunteering for a pro-life organization. He had asked Duke to ask our Blessed Mother if he should stop that work and change to a different ministry. My impression was that Duke was not comfortable asking Mary about that. Duke suggested to the individual that he should pray for guidance. A week or two later I overheard Duke saying that he had apologized to the individual for telling him to pray about it. Mary, in her next visit to Duke, instructed him to tell that individual to continue with his work in the pro-life organization."

"I remember Duke telling us at prayer group about a visit that he had had earlier that day while at work in the library. I thought that it was the Archangel Gabriel, but it could have been St. Michael. Duke talked about how big and powerful he appeared."

"One time we were praying inside to the right of the main altar. It was winter. After the rosary, Duke told all of us that Jesus had been there and put his hands on the top of Sissy's head. Duke said he wasn't sure why Jesus did that. Weeks later, Sissy told us that she had cancer. Later, when she went for more tests, the cancer was gone. She lived a few more years after that."

"It was September, and we were going to meet inside because the birds and bells were a distraction to some of the members of the prayer group. Earlier that day, Mary told Duke she wanted us to meet outside by the Grotto in the garden. As we came outside, there was a strong smell of roses. None of the roses in the garden were blooming. The only flowers in sight were plastic! My father, who was over ninety years old at the time, and had lost his senses of smell and taste, remarked on the strong smell of roses. Mary appeared to Duke, in a remarkable way that evening."

From Claire:

"Since Mary called OLHSC "her house", sometimes we would walk into the building and say, 'Mother, we're home!'"

"I remember when Duke's knees were hurting badly, and it was painful for him to walk. However, he would kneel for a long time on the rough stones, or directly in front of the Our Lady of Lourdes' Statue during our prayers and Mary's visits."

"One evening, as we were assembling for rosary, we were laughing about something; I don't remember what. Later, after we had finished praying, Duke told us that Mary had appeared and wanted us to know how much she enjoyed our laughter."

"I remember when Vi told us that her father had helped to build the Lourdes' Grotto in the courtyard of OLHSC. As the buildings were completed in 1923, it was probably around that time that he laid the stones for the grotto. It made that place even more special for us, as she was a regular member of our group until she died."

"We watched our granddaughter, Ella, every-other Thursday evening, and she would come with us for rosary often. When she was about a year old, I would put her in a stroller, and walk her up and down the long dark hallway near the chapel where we were praying. She would fall asleep within a few minutes, and I would take her back into the room where everyone was assembled. Ella would stay asleep until our last prayer, and then wake up peacefully. I imagined that Our Blessed Mother was rocking her as she slept. As Ella got older, she would curl up into my lap as we prayed, or go to the children's section of the library to look at books. She never complained about the seventy minutes of prayer that it took to complete four mysteries. She seemed to enjoy the quiet time, and soon learned the prayers. She also enjoyed the gardens before we began our rosary, playing 'Hide and Seek' with me behind the statues. One time, when we were in the garden, she said she saw Jesus standing with his arms outstretched and smiling at her."

Our Rosary group was very important to us throughout those fourteen years. We relied on each other for support, prayers, and encouragement. It is wonderful how God sends just the right people into our lives, at just the right time, to strengthen us, guide us, and help us on our way to heaven.

7

Messages, Glimpses and Other Wonders

Our Blessed Mother told Duke, in 2001, that he was in "The School of Mary." She had a lot to teach him. Duke said that after she came with a message, he would find a piece of paper and a pen and pray to the Holy Spirit to guide him as he wrote. If you examined the collection of these hand-written messages, you would notice that they were written on any odd piece of paper Duke could grab quickly; one is even on a piece of card-board!

Sometimes, Our Blessed Mother gave Duke messages for members of our family and people we knew. Those were never shared through email or the website. We gave these messages to the intended parties, and I never kept a record of them. Often, I never read them myself.

Mary also gave Duke private messages that he didn't share with anyone; not even with me. He told me that he carried a heavy burden with some of those private messages.

Most of the messages were given "For all who will listen." They range in dates from July 10, 2001 until June 28, 2012. Duke died August 20, 2012. They include seventy messages from Mary, twenty messages from Jesus, one message from St. Therese, one message from the Archangel Gabriel, one message from Father Slavko Barbaric, and one message from the Holy Spirit.

So, now, as you read these messages, you are also in the school of Mary. Following Father Ray's advice, I suggest that you read one message at a time. Give yourself a day or two between messages to let the ideas settle into your mind and heart. Don't read just words. Think about each sentence and how it applies to your life. You might want to go back to Chapter Five and re-read the messages we gave to Father Ray Favret before reading more messages in this chapter.

I have prayed about which messages and glimpses to include in this book. My hope is that they touch you and your loved ones, as they have touched me.

September 11, 2001, was the day we were attacked, and so many American lives were lost. Our normal rosary group of seven or eight people expanded that night to about thirty. Everyone was on edge about the future of our lives and our country. We seemed to need prayer above all else. The following message was given to Duke from Our Blessed Mother for "All Who Will Listen," eight days later.

9/19/01

"My Angel,

I send you my motherly love and blessings. My heart aches for all my children who have suffered due to the recent tragedies. I, too, have shed many tears. Through this darkest of hours there shines a great light. A mighty river of prayers is flowing before the throne of God. I tell you the truth, I have never before seen such an outpouring of prayers throughout the world. In every nation, people of every faith are lifting their eyes and their ears to the Father for comfort and guidance. Through my tears my heart sings with joy!

Continue to pray for peace; peace in your hearts, peace in the hearts of all mankind, and peace for the world. Pray that my Son will lead the souls of my dear departed children to the light of His presence. Pray that His love and peace is felt in the hearts of all those who are grieving. Pray that the leaders throughout the world act out of justice and not hatred or revenge.

Tell my children all that I have spoken. Know that the Father is with His children and He holds you in the palm of His hand. Thank you for having responded to my call."

Other messages from Our Blessed Mother follow:

10/26/01

"My Dearest Angel,

As always, I send you my Motherly love and blessings.

The Father desires that all of His children should live their lives filled with peace and joy. Do not dwell upon tomorrow, for tomorrow will take care of itself. Live each day in joy, knowing that the Father loves each of His children with unimaginable love. Live your lives in accordance with God's will, my children. It is only there that you will find true peace and happiness.

Do you imagine that the Father asks His children to follow His will for His sake? No! It is because He knows that only by doing so can His children be truly happy. Who to know better than He, what His creation requires for true happiness?

There is much beauty to be seen in God's creation, but there is no beauty that can compare to a soul that is in harmony with God's will. Your soul will burst forth with a beauty that even the most exquisite roses cannot rival. Your heart will sing with a glorious chorus of peace and harmony.

My little ones, you must pray, pray, pray! Only through a life of prayer can you obtain harmony with the Father's will. Only through prayer can you develop a relationship with my Son and the Father. I tell you the truth, my children, there is no greater love than the love that the Father has for His children!

My angel, tell this message to all who will listen. Thank you for having responded to my call."

11/20/01

"My Angel,

I send you my Motherly love and blessings. It is my heart's desire to lead all of my children towards greater holiness. Live your faith! Let your light shine for all of the world to see. If you deny my Son before your fellow man, He will deny you before the Father.

Hunger for those things which feed the spirit: prayer, Holy Mass, Holy Communion, and the Holy Scriptures. Shun the evil that this world has to offer. Satan is very cunning and he will lead you astray if he can!

Prayer is your greatest defense. Pray for the Holy Spirit to come into your hearts. Pray for the love and the peace that my Son so willingly offers. Surrender your will to my Son and walk in Grace.

Tell all who will listen. Thank you for responding to my call."

12/2/01

"My Dearest Angel,

During this most joyous of seasons, as another year draws to an end, I wish for all of my children to bear in mind my messages. It is my heart's desire that all my children truly live my messages so that my Son can present my children before the Father as a perfect gift.

My little ones, you must pray without ceasing. Pray from your hearts. Pray to Jesus. Talk to Him. Surrender your wills to Him. Let Jesus become your constant companion. He will bear you up and carry your burden. Without prayer you can never hope to conquer Satan.

Appreciate the gift that is so freely given to you through the Holy Eucharist. Always receive the Holy Eucharist with reverence and joy. So many of my children do not receive the gifts and graces that the Holy Eucharist embodies because they do not approach the Lord's table with the proper reverence.

Throughout the ages it has caused me great sadness because my children do not study the Holy Scriptures as they should. The Holy Scriptures are your spiritual food. Without prayer and the searching of the Holy Scriptures your soul will wither and die!

It is my heart's desire that all of my children should fast on bread and water on Wednesdays and Fridays. Begin your fasting at sunset and end your fasting at sunset[8]. Fasting helps the soul focus on the Father. Fasting is a gift of sacrifice that is offered up to the Father. Your Mother offers up your prayers and fasting on your behalf when I intercede to the Lord. Little do you realize, my dearest ones, that prayer, along with fasting, is the greatest force in all of God's creation.

I urge all of my children to go to Confession at least once a month. Do not deny yourselves the graces that Confession has to offer! My Son aches in His heart to draw you close to His side, and to hold you in His arms. But in order for Him to do so, you must first confess your sins and implore His forgiveness.

Now is the time of great graces and gifts. The Holy Spirit is being sent out unto the world as He never has been before. Prepare your hearts to receive Him and all the gifts and graces that the Father so freely offers. Consecrate your hearts to Jesus. Do not harden your hearts to God's Holy Spirit. Do not delay, for God's Spirit will not always strive with mankind.

Remember to keep the Lord's Day holy. When you leave Holy Mass, my children, do not go about your business as if the Lord's Day was just like any other day. Rather, spend the Lord's Day in communion with God as it was intended to be. Study the Holy Scriptures and reflect on God's love and mercy.

Finally, my Angel, I tell you the truth! The hour of the Son of God is truly at hand. Be ever vigilant. Do not be caught asleep. Trim your lamps and keep your countenances lifted unto the Lord.

My Angel, tell all who will listen. Go in peace to love and serve the Lord. Praise be to Jesus! Thank you for having responded to my call."

1/9/03

"My Angel,

Satan is becoming increasingly cunning and deceitful. He is employing his full arsenal, for I tell you the truth, my little ones, this is truly war! [Do] you ask how you can stand firm against this onslaught? Turn to the Holy Scriptures, my precious ones, and read Ephesians 6:10-18.[9] Follow God's Holy words and you will surely triumph!

Know that I will never truly leave you. I will be in your heart and you in mine. I will wrap you in the mantle of my love and protection. Be glad and rejoice, my children. Stand firm in your faith and your devotion to God. God's love and grace will be with you ever unto the end of the world.

My angel, tell my message to all who will listen. Pray constantly for the conversion of your brothers and sisters and for God's mercy upon the world.

Thank you for having responded to my call. Go in peace to love and serve the Lord. Praise Jesus!"

> **"Finally, draw your strength from the Lord and from His mighty power. Put on the armor of God so that you may be able to stand firm against the tactics of the devil. For our struggle is not with flesh and blood but with principalities, with the powers, with the world rulers of this present darkness, with the evil spirits of the heavens. Therefore, put on the armor of God, that you may be able to resist on the evil day, and having done everything, to hold your ground. So, stand fast with your loins girded in truth clothed with righteousness as a breastplate, and your feet shod in readiness for the gospel of peace. In all circumstances, hold faith as a shield, to quench all [the] flaming arrows of the evil one. And take the helmet of salvation and the sword of the Spirit, which is the word of God."**
>
> **Eph 6: 10-18**

Initially, Duke only heard Our Blessed Mother's voice, but soon after we returned home from Medjugorje, he began to see her as well. When we asked what she looked like, sometimes he would get testy, and say, "It's not important what she looks like. It's her message that's important."

One time, Mary scolded him for reacting this way. She said, "People want to know what you see. They are curious. And ladies like to know how I am dressed. Tell them I am wearing my golden sandals today."

This is the description I remember he shared with us once: "I think she is about nineteen years old, but I am bad at guessing ages. She is small, like Claire. She has black hair and violet eyes and an olive complexion.

She has high cheek bones. She is standing on a cloud, and says, 'Praise be to Jesus,' when she first comes. Her eyes project all of her love. They are so beautiful and hold most of my attention." Sometimes he would tell us what she was wearing, but usually not. Her clothing seemed to vary with seasons or feasts. He was reluctant to talk about how she looked and we would have to be persistent to get any information.

In August of 2001, shortly after we had arrived home from Medjugorje, Our Blessed Mother asked Duke if he would like to see the day Father Slavko "was born into heaven." Duke, of course, said, "Yes." Then she gave him a glimpse of the scene. Duke said he saw an old man[10] approaching Jesus. He knelt down and bowed his head. Jesus put his hands on Father Slavko's shoulders and said, "Well done, my good and faithful servant." Then Father Slavko stood up as a healthy-looking young man. Duke told me, through tears, that all he wanted was the same reception from Jesus on the day he entered heaven.

On Christmas, 2001, Duke, Alicia (our daughter, then twenty years old) and I were in our family room praying the rosary. Mary appeared to Duke dressed in white with golden trim, holding the infant Jesus. She asked Duke, "Would you like to hold your baby Brother?" Duke said, "Yes." She leaned over and put baby Jesus into Duke's out-stretched arms. At that point, Alicia and I stopped praying and just watched Duke cradling a baby that we could not see. I could only guess what was happening. Duke said later, that he put his finger into baby Jesus' fist, as he held on tightly. This lasted only a minute or two. Then Mary bent over and took baby Jesus back into her arms.

Mary told Duke that it was sad for her when she recalled that the only cloth she had to wrap her newborn infant in was stiff and scratchy, so that it left red marks on His skin. She said, through tears, that the cloth she wrapped her crucified Son in was of the finest weave, and it was very soft.

After Mary was gone, Duke looked at Alicia and I and told us what had just happened. He made us promise not to tell anyone about this experience, as it was too personal and unbelievable. Years later, he shared this with some of our rosary group members, and now I am sharing it with you!

Between 2001 and 2003, Duke was granted three glimpses of what could happen to us after death; one of heaven, one of purgatory, and one of hell. Duke said that the one thing that stood out to him about heaven was the brilliant colors. He saw people walking around in white robes, but he saw no one he recognized. Mary walked with him a short while, pointing out how wonderful it was. Another time, he saw Our Blessed Mother sitting on a rock in heaven, and gently splashing her feet in a cool stream. Jesus came up behind her and put his hands on her shoulders. She touched one of His hands and then put her other hand on an empty space on the rock. She turned to Duke and said, "I am saving this spot for you."

He didn't see much in Purgatory. Duke said it was obscured by clouds or mist. He did hear a woman pleading, "Michael, pray for me." He thought Michael might be her husband, still alive on earth.

St. Michael, the Archangel, took Duke to see hell. Duke said he was terrified and hid behind St. Michael, clinging to him. He was afraid to look, but he heard the souls in hell cursing God.

On Trinity Sunday, 6/15/03 Duke reported that he had been given his first message from Jesus. He was very reticent about sharing this, even with me. He said it was hard enough to tell others he was receiving messages from Mary, but it was quite another thing to tell others that he had received a message from Jesus. I think it took about a week for Duke to get enough courage to ask me to send the following message out to those on our email list.

Introduction from Duke: "Mary told me about a month ago, that soon I would be receiving messages from her Son. I received my first message from our precious Jesus during the Mass celebrating the Feast of the Holy Trinity."

6/15/03

"My Beloved Brother,

During My life on earth, in My every action and My every word, I truly reflected the Father's love. Before I returned to My Father's side, I established My Church on earth to spread the Gospel of the Father's love and mercy. Also, as I promised, once I did return to My Father's Kingdom, I sent the Holy Spirit to provide guidance and instruction.

And yet, still so many of our Father's children wander in darkness and not knowing the Father's love. Those of you who love Me, must truly be the light of the world. Let the Father's love shine through you for all to see. Tell your brothers and sisters of My love for them. Tell them how the Father longs for them to return to His love.

Satan would have them believe that the standard that has been set is impossible to achieve, so why ever try. Tell them that this is simply not so! All that they need to do is chose to love. Love is the key that unlocks the door leading to righteousness. Pray for one another. Love one another as I have loved you. Love the Father with all of your heart and soul. Pray for those that would do you harm. For I tell you the truth, this is how you will be judged; on how well you loved.

Thank you for having responded to our Mother's call. Through your willingness to share Her messages, many souls are being won for the Father.

Finally, tell your brothers and sisters how I long for them to walk with Me and to talk to Me. I yearn for a close relationship with all of My brothers and sisters. If they could only truly understand how I love them! Go in peace, my beloved brother, knowing that I am with you always."

7/20/03

"My Beloved Brother,

Our Mother has taken you by the hand and led you to Me. It is our Mother's heart's desire to lead all of her children to Me. There is nothing to be added or taken away from what she has spoken unto you. You have been given the road map to salvation. Heed what she has revealed unto you!

Now, it is My joy to aid you on your spiritual journey by taking you by the hand and leading you to Our Father. As you begin to know Me better, you will begin to truly experience My love. My love and the Father's love for you are one and the same, thus, through Me, you will come to love our Father even as I do. Your heart will be overflowing with His love. Once you have the Father's love in your heart you cannot but love Him in return, for love begets love. This love will create in you a great hunger to know the Father even more deeply. Out of love, you will be eager to do His Will. Your life will become one of prayer and praise. Your faith will become strong. Lucifer and all of his fallen angels will tremble at the sight.

This is what I desire for all of My brothers and sisters. Come unto Me and let Me lead you to true peace and happiness. Do not be led astray by Lucifer's lies and deceptions.

Of all of the Father's creations, mankind is the one creation that the Father holds dearest and closest to His heart. That is why Lucifer despises you so! That is why he is intent upon your ruin and destruction.

You were created to be children of the Eternal Light. When the Father breathed the breath of life into man, He imparted His love and tenderness to the fullest. Come unto Me and walk with Me. Claim the gift of salvation and eternal life that I gained for you. We love you more than you can ever begin to understand. We desire only your peace and true happiness. I cry out to My lost sheep, but so many do not hear or heed My call. I am with you always. I am waiting with outstretched arms to welcome you home.

Go in peace, my beloved brother, knowing that I am with you always."

I've often been asked if I was ever jealous of Duke for having all of these wonderful experiences. I can honestly say that most of the time I just felt very privileged and blessed to be with him when he was talking to a visitor from Heaven.

However, there was one time I thought it should have been me and not him. It was during the first year after our trip to Medjugorje when so much was happening quickly. We were scheduled to make a presentation one evening, and Duke was very nervous about it. As he was getting ready, standing in front of the bathroom mirror shaving, he had a glimpse he didn't understand. He was transported to a courtyard with a large cross near the center. He stood still while two nuns carried a third sickly nun in a bed sheet, like a hammock, and approached him. He said they stopped walking when the sick nun motioned to Duke to come to her. When he did, she blessed him in French. Then Duke was back standing in front of the mirror.

Duke asked me if I knew what had just happened to him. I certainly did! I popped in a VHS tape that I'd had for years. It was a documentary on the life of St. Therese, the Little Flower. I fast-forwarded to the part where a nun was giving a tour of the convent courtyard in Lisieux.

Duke jumped out of his chair and ran to the screen and pointed. "Yes! That's where I was. She was here, and I was there, and that is the cross I saw. Who is she?"

"Sweetheart," I said with tears in my eyes. "She is my sister in heaven. She is St. Therese, the Little Flower of Lisieux. Don't you remember? I told you, she is my favorite saint. I took her name when I was confirmed." I showed him several photos of St. Therese from one of my books. Celine, her sister, had taken most of the photos.

Duke said, "That doesn't look like her. The nun I saw looked very sick and shriveled up." I told him that they must have been transporting her from her cell to the infirmary, shortly before her death. She had been sick for a long time, and couldn't eat anything, even the Holy Eucharist, in her last days.

St. Therese came to him another time, when Duke was getting frustrated that he wasn't doing enough for God. She spoke to him in English this time and told him, "Just take baby steps."

On 5/25/06, St. Therese gave him the following message to share with others.

"My Beloved Brother in Christ,

I wish to extend to my brothers and sisters some insight into spirituality.

So many of my brothers and sisters seem to be confused and lost. It is my heart's desire that this message is helpful.

You must know that spirituality is something that you cannot earn or acquire through your own actions and deeds alone. You must ask God to come into your heart. You have the choice. You have free will. The Father will not enter into your heart until you ask him to enter. At that moment, if you are truly sincere, your growth begins. You will feel a great peace come over you. The Holy Spirit will begin to speak to your heart. Again, you must pray from your heart before the Holy Spirit will begin to extend unto you His gifts.

You must pray to the Lord every day. Although the Holy Rosary is a powerful prayer, and absolutely should be said every day, you also need to spend time with the Lord on an intimate level. Look deep into your soul and recognize your faults and weaknesses. Hold them up to the Lord and ask Him to remove them from your heart and mind. He will! What joy you will receive as your faults fade away. You will sing for joy! As you spend time with Jesus, you will begin to know Him on a personal level. Your love for Him will grow and grow as you begin to grasp His love for you.

You must study the Holy Scriptures also, every day. Before you begin, pray to the Holy Spirit for understanding and enlightenment. Then, as you read God's word, the words will leap from the page and become alive for you. You will begin to understand the Father's love for you and love will grow in your heart. You will develop a thirst and hunger to learn more.

Fasting, if done from the heart joyfully, will open your heart and mind to the Holy Spirit. The graces and blessings that you receive will be many.

Go to Holy Mass as often as you possibly can. There you will be led to Christ's table and through the sacrament of the Eucharist, you will receive our Lord! It is such an intimate experience. It fills my soul with awe!

Confession is a wonderful gift. To receive it spiritually you must have a pure heart. If your heart is not pure, the gifts from the Holy Spirit cannot be obtained. Go to Confession with a joyful and humble heart and receive the Father's Grace.

Spirituality is having your heart and the Father's heart joined as one. It is a life-long journey and is most often obtained step by step. Do not be discouraged if you stumble and fall. The Father is waiting with open arms to receive you and to forgive. Place your feet back on the path and journey towards righteousness. It is not an easy path. Many times, you will have crosses that you will have to bear. However, the joy of striving to be one with the Father will overshadow anything that you have to bear.

Go in peace to love and to serve the Lord. Let your light shine for all to see. You are children of the Father. Receive His love, peace, grace and blessings.

All glory be to the Father now and forever."

That same day, St. Therese gave Duke a personal message for me. Part of what she said was, "Please tell her that she can rest assured that I love her, too Her mother is very proud of her…". It still takes my breath away to read this letter. How blessed I have been!

During Duke's glimpses, he seemed to be transported to the place and time of the event, rather than just observing from a distance. He said he could smell the animals, feel the heat, and see details that one would not normally observe if watching a video.

The glimpses that made the most impressions on me were when he described details as if he was standing very close. When Joseph was pushed back into the street by the burly innkeeper because there was no room for them in the inn, Duke showed me on his arm, exactly where Joseph had scraped his arm on the rocks as he fell backward into the street. In another glimpse Duke described how dirty the hem of Mary's robe had become from the floor of the cave in which Jesus was born.

His favorite glimpse was of Mary and Jesus at the wedding feast of Cana. Duke loved to describe the silent interplay between their expressions, especially when Mary said, "Do whatever he tells you." Duke said that Jesus just rolled his eyes like any son would when he realized that his Mom was going to get her way. Duke said it was all done in an atmosphere of love and respect. He enjoyed watching them have so much fun at the wedding.

Another one of his favorite glimpses was of St. Joseph as he cradled baby Jesus, shortly after He was born. Joseph repeated, through happy tears, "He's so beautiful. He's so beautiful."

Glimpses of the Passion of the Christ were not so easy for him to witness. Sometimes Duke would cry when he described what he had just seen. He said that by the time Jesus had been nailed to the cross He had been so brutally beaten that He didn't even look like a human being.

A glimpse Duke had in early 2002 occurred a couple of hours before one of our scheduled presentations. Duke said he was suddenly transferred into a boat rocking in a storm. He said the waves were washing over the boat and the men in the boat were all trying to bail the water out with whatever they had available. Duke said he was wet, cold, and very afraid.

Eventually, someone woke Jesus up, and He calmed the storm. Then, Duke was back in his home as suddenly as he had gone.

One time, on Valentine's day, Duke came home with a beautiful butterfly pendant. He told me that he had been in the jewelry shop to pick up his watch after it had been repaired. He said that Mary spoke to him while he was in the store. She said, "Turn right, turn left, bend down. There, buy that for Claire to remind her of my butterfly kisses."

He did as he was told, and after I opened my gift, he said to me, "Now what does she mean by her 'butterfly kisses?" I told him of the time, in the summer of 1996, when I was painting our deck. Chris was in Costa Rica, and hadn't called, as directed, for forty-four days. Our Blessed Mother had eased my worries by sending a butterfly to kiss me. I also said, "If I had told you at that time, you would have thought I was crazy, right?" He said, "I probably would have."

There were also private visitations that provided Duke with personal instruction or direction. One was from St. Mother Theresa of Calcutta. Duke said she looked just as she does in the photos of her; old and scary. He had been volunteering sixteen hours a week in the library at Our Lady of the Holy Spirit Center at that time. He decided to do more volunteer work, so he interviewed with the St. Vincent de Paul Society. He was ready to commit some time to that ministry when St. Mother Theresa visited him in his sleep, shortly after his interview. He said she put a boney finger close to his face and said something like "You'd better be sure about this. Once you say you are going to do something, you'd better do it. You can't say you are too tired or feel too bad to go. You better just go!" He decided that the sixteen hours in the library were enough, given his poor health. He didn't want another scolding!

Mary also taught Duke how to pray the rosary. I had been taught to think about each part of the mystery as I said the "Hail Mary's." Mary said she would prefer that we meditate on the mystery before we begin the "Our Father." Then, when we say the prayers, we should pray from the heart, thinking about each word of each prayer. Often, when Duke and I would pray together, he would slow me down by saying, "I can't pray from the heart when you go so fast." So, my protestant-raised husband taught me how to say a proper rosary!

One time, Our Lady was talking to Duke about the time Jesus selected Peter as the head of the Church. Mary said she thought that John would have been a better choice because Peter was so impetuous and would leap into a situation without thinking it through. She said that Jesus knew Peter's heart, however, and that he was tenacious and a natural leader. Once Peter made up his mind to do something, he could not be dissuaded. It took those qualities to keep the early Church together. Mary told Duke, "You remind me of Peter, but you need many more prayers."

Duke was also privileged to see Jesus' face in the Sacred Host during the consecration of the Holy Mass. This happened only one time that I know of. Another time he saw Our Lady kneeling before the altar during the consecration. I remember he whispered to me at that time, "Mary is on the altar now."

We did several talks those first few years. I did not keep a journal of these events, so I don't have an accurate account. My estimate is about twelve per year. Each time, after we spoke and took questions, I passed around a paper for people to provide me with their emails if they wanted copies of the messages as Duke received them. We had a list of about one hundred people with whom we were staying in touch.

www.dukesallwhowilllisten.blogspot.com is the place to find more messages today.

We were truly blessed to be so close to Jesus and Our Blessed Mother for so many years. But with great blessings also comes great responsibilities. Mary told us that where she is, Satan is not far behind. Sometimes we didn't feel strong enough for all of the challenges that we were facing. Sometimes we struggled to keep our eyes on Jesus.

8

Changed Lives

I've often been asked how our lives changed since July 2001. Well, there were a lot of changes, and some weren't easily understood or appreciated.

Duke's health continued to deteriorate and he experienced a lot of pain. In addition to the migraines, he began suffering from back pain. He saw a specialist who tried shots of steroids into his spine. That procedure was so painful that I could hear Duke screaming while I sat the waiting room. Each treatment alleviated some pain for a few days, and then he was back on pain medication. After five injections, both Duke and the doctor decided to give up on those shots.

Duke tried wearing a TENS unit attached to his back for a year or so, but he said that did not do much to relieve the pain either.

He had seen two back specialists who could not offer us much hope. We finally found a third doctor who thought he could help. Duke endured two major surgeries that involved placing eighteen rods and numerous pins into his back. This finally solved the back pain, but then, soon after, Duke's knees began hurting.

One orthopedic surgeon thought he could fix both knees with partial knee replacements. He did one at a time, but it wasn't more than two years before each of those partials either dislocated or broke.

One time, Duke was bending over, shining his shoes, right before our annual Christmas party, when he experienced a sudden and severe pain in his knee. My son, Chris, drove Duke to the emergency room, while I stayed home to greet our guests. The emergency room doctor told Duke he had just sprained a muscle. He gave him pain pills and sent him home. The next day, after the pain pills wore off, Duke was still experiencing terrible pain. I took Duke back to the hospital, and this time they took x-rays. They scheduled surgery for December 26 to replace the broken pieces of his partial with a total knee replacement. The next year, the doctor replaced his other partial, when it went bad, with a full knee replacement.

After the second full knee replacement, we were in Ireland on vacation with my cousin, her husband, and two priests from their Diocese. After dinner one night, Duke experienced extreme pain in his right knee. The younger priest tried to help him hobble back to the hotel, but Duke couldn't walk at all. Father ran to the hotel and returned with a wheel chair. After an hour of trying to relieve his pain with ice, I asked the front desk clerk to call for a doctor. The doctor arrived, gave Duke a shot of something for the pain, and called an ambulance. I rode with him in the ambulance for forty minutes to the nearest hospital. By then Duke had passed out. They took him into the treatment area immediately while I sat in the waiting room for three hours. They said he had a serious strep infection in his knee, and would need to be in the hospital for at least eight days while they drained and treated the infected area. The Irish doctor told me that the infection had damaged his knee replacement and he would need another one eventually.

When we returned home, it took about four months to rid his body of the strep infection. The doctor then removed the damaged pieces of his knee and replaced them with a spacer. Duke experienced six more months of painful walking before his final knee replacement surgery. Five days later, Duke died suddenly from a blood clot that caused a heart attack.

Another way our lives were changed, in the midst of the messages and glimpses, was financially. Eight months after we got home from Medjugorje, on April 1, 2002, Duke lost his job. He began looking for another job right away, but could not find one comparable to the jobs he had worked most of his adult life.

He worked a couple of minimum wage jobs over the next few years, and then, due to his constant pain and surgeries, couldn't work at all. He tried applying for disability, but he was denied benefits.

As we had a rather high mortgage, we sold our house in West Chester as soon as possible. Then we bought a modest home in Springfield Township. Not too many months after that, Duke's expensive sports car was totaled by a deer. He ended up driving a four-thousand-dollar car to his job at United Dairy Farmers, cleaning bathrooms and scooping ice cream.

Duke and Claire are carrying the cross on the Via Dolorosa in Jerusalem, February 2006.

Within two years of our trip to Medjugorje, Duke had lost his prestigious job, his nice home, and his sports car. He asked Mary "Why? Why?" She said he needed lessons in humility, and that he needed to be "tested in the fire". Duke wasn't sure what that meant, but he did feel under fire.

He certainly got lessons in humility, and they were hard lessons. He also learned that material possessions were not as important as he once thought. His Mother Mary taught him what was important--- and it wasn't owning fine things.

I mentioned this before in another chapter, but it bears repeating. We felt temped by Satan, after July 2001, to divorce or separate. I remember one time I was particularly upset with Duke about our finances. In my mind (encouraged by Satan, I'm sure) it was his fault that we were in such economic distress.

During rosary that night in our home, Our Blessed Mother came and spoke to Duke as he gazed upward. At one point in their conversation, Duke looked right at me and said, "Don't be angry with him. He loves you so much." It was Duke's voice, but I knew it was Mary's message to me. After Our Blessed Mother left, Duke told me that while he had been talking to Mary, she said to him, "I'm sorry you are so worried about money." Duke said, "Then, she looked right at you, Claire, and said something, but I don't know what she said." Through tears, I told him what she had said. That never happened to us before or since, but it was a very powerful lesson for both of us.

Another time Duke was visiting his sister in Shelbyville, Indiana. I was upset with him, again, and told him not to come home. He came home about six hours later. As I heard his car pull into the driveway, I rehearsed these words, "What don't you understand about, 'Don't come home?'" Immediately I heard a voice in my heart say to me, "What don't you understand about, 'Till death do us part?'" So, when he came into our bedroom, I just embraced him and said, "I'm sorry."

> **"Some Pharisees approached Jesus, and testing him, saying, 'Is it lawful for a man to divorce his wife for any cause whatever?' He said in reply, 'Have you not read that from the beginning *the Creator made them male and female* and said, *for this reason a man shall leave his father and mother and be joined to his wife, and the two shall become one flesh?* So, they are no longer two, but one flesh. Therefore, what God has joined together man must not separate."**
> **Matt 19:3-6**

Another one of Duke's great trials had to do with his addiction to cigarettes and nicotine. One of the doctors he saw for his back pain said that his lungs were in bad shape from forty years of smoking. In the 1980's and 90's he had tried nicotine patches, hypnosis, and even acupuncture. Finally, he tried nicotine gum. That helped, but then he began to lose his teeth. He was never able to stop smoking completely, but he was able to slow down quite a bit before he died.

"No trial has come to you but what is human. God is faithful and will not let you be tried beyond your strength; but with trial He will also provide a way out, so that you may be able to bear it."
1Corinthians 10:13

With all of the challenges, however, our lives changed in many good ways. Before I retired, I attended 6:30 am daily mass alone and got to work by 7:15. After I retired, I took contract work in order to maintain medical insurance and supplemental income. This afforded me a more flexible schedule. When Duke worked third shift at UDF, he would get off work at 7:30 a.m., so we could meet at church for the 8:00 am mass before I left for work. It was a wonderful way to start our day together.

Before July 2001, I said a five-decade rosary each evening alone. Afterwards, we said a fifteen or twenty-decade rosary together, as recommended by Our Blessed Mother. We would encourage each other to pray from the heart. Sometimes we would pause and share our thoughts on the mystery as the Holy Spirit inspired us to do. Often, Mary would visit us during our prayers.

Before our trip to Medjugorje, neither of us had ever been to Adoration. I had never been raised with any knowledge of this devotion. After we came home, we began searching for an adoration chapel, and found one that we loved at Our Lady of the Holy Spirit Center. Duke signed up for an hour in the middle of the night, and I preferred the afternoon. We both loved this newly discovered devotion. I continue to pray before the Blessed Sacrament at least once a week.

Duke and I had not been going to confession as often as Our Blessed Mother wished us to. It was the toughest part of her requests for us to do. One of my favorite memories of Duke going to confession was when we attended a Marion Conference in South Bend, Indiana on the Notre Dame College campus. Duke returned to his seat like a little child. He was literally dancing and beaming. He said a boulder had been lifted from his shoulders. He was so grateful to the Franciscan Priest who had guided him lovingly, through a difficult confession. I have learned since, that the more often I go to confession (The Sacrament of Reconciliation), the easier and more beneficial it becomes.

> **"Fear not, I am with you; be not dismayed; I am your God. I will strengthen you, and help you, and uphold you with my right hand of justice."**
> **Isaiah 41:10**

Eighteen months before our trip to Medjugorje, I began fasting on bread and water each Wednesday and Friday, while Duke ate normal meals. After our trip, we fasted together from sundown to sundown. I remember one time, Duke took a bite of his bread, gave me a big smile and said, "Yum. Great meal, Honey." Often on Fridays, we would watch the sunset and then head out to dinner, to celebrate the end of our fast.

As we learned that our treasures in heaven are more precious than our treasures on Earth, we became less and less concerned about material possessions.

We became more aware of Satan's subtle attacks to make us unhappy and we were more often able to resist the evil thoughts he put into our minds.

So, through all of the wonders, messages and glimpses, we had many trials. However, and this is a big however, Our Blessed Mother and Our Lord and Savior, continued to help us through all of these hardships. Without our faith, we would never have been able to endure, keep our marriage strong, and continue our process of conversion. We learned the importance of prayer from the heart. We learned that life on this Earth is but a drop in the ocean of eternity. We learned that conversion is not a one-time event; it is a slow process of continuous prayer and infusion of Grace. Almost twenty years later, I am still learning in the "School of Mary."

9

Through Mary's Eyes

I recorded most of the messages Duke received from 2001-2012, (except for the personal messages) and shared these through email with about one hundred people. I was encouraged by our rosary group to record the glimpses as well. I was not sure how to share these, but soon, I began to compose meditations for the rosary, since many of the glimpses paralleled the mysteries. I shared these with a few people, primarily those who attended our weekly rosary prayers.

At some point around 2003, a Marriage Encounter friend, Andrew, who was a wiz with the internet, developed a web page for me. I was able to post the messages and rosary meditations on that platform. I began to feel, however, that this was not reaching enough people. So, the urge to write a story about Mary's life, as seen through Duke's glimpses, began to take shape. My initial plan was to post this story on the web as well. Before long, however, I began to get the idea of writing a book. I was working about fifty hours a week as a school administrator at that time, so I didn't have many free hours to dedicate to this project.

Before sitting down to write anything, I would pray a rosary, read the bible section related to the scene, and sometimes reference maps and google earth, to get a sense of geography and perspective.

After writing a chapter, I would give it to Duke to proof. Often, he would make a suggestion for a minor change, but a few times I had to change several pages based on his memory of the glimpse.

One chapter included a rainstorm. I had described Mary's house with rain gutters all around, leading to a rain barrel, which the inhabitants and visitors could use as a source of water for drinking and washing. Duke said that he never saw such a contrivance as a part of her house, and he didn't think there was enough rain in that region to make it practical. I did some research about the climate of Ephesus and surrounding areas, and discovered he was right. So, I had to rewrite the scene about the rainstorm and the source for water. That changed many scenes in the book, including Mary's walk to the well from her home on the hill.

Another time he found fault with the final chapter about the Assumption. I had written that Gabriel arrived with his arms full of flowers from heaven. I described, in great detail, the colors and delightful smells emanating from the bouquet.

Duke said that this part of my story was all wrong. He said that Mary had picked her own flowers from the hillside near her home, to lay on her mat for John to discover. Duke described those flowers as tiny, white, and starshaped. So, I rewrote the entire scene to be more in line with what he had seen in his glimpse of the event.

Soon after that, we were at Our Lady of the Holy Spirit Center waiting for our rosary group to arrive. Duke waited in the library, and I went out into the garden to pray alone by the grotto. I sat on a bench, and before I began praying, I glanced down and saw a clump of tiny, white, starshaped flowers growing next to my bench. I grabbed one of those flowers and ran back into the library. I asked Duke if what I had just picked was the same flower that he saw Mary gathering from outside her home. He said it was. Then we began doing research, and found out, to our delight, that this flower is called "The Star of Bethlehem!" The next year, I found this plant growing alongside the statue of Our Lady of Grace in our back yard. We had never planted it. We figured it was one of those common plants that naturally propagate from wind or bird activity, and that this was a special gift from our Blessed Mother.

One time, Duke was reading the chapter about Luke as a young boy. He had never had any glimpses of these events, as I had conjured them on my own. I had almost seen (or was it a dream?) the drama with the Roman soldiers in the marketplace, when Mary hid Luke inside her mantle. I had done some research regarding Luke, and discovered traditional beliefs that Luke painted portraits of Jesus and Mary, and was a physician. I wanted to write about the source of his knowledge of healing and painting, and how he came to know Our Blessed Mother so well. Duke said that if he had not seen any glimpses of Luke, I should not include him in my story. So, on Duke's request, I deleted all references to Luke as a child.

That same night, Our Blessed Mother talked to Duke and told him that, "This story is between Claire and I." So, embarrassed by this minor scolding, he told me to put the story of the young Luke back into the book, and he would not second guess me again about story lines he had not seen in glimpses. I rewrote the chapters from memory, as I had deleted my only copy, but I sense that the second version was better than the first. So, in the end, it all worked out.

After Duke looked at each chapter, and approved, I gave it to members of our rosary group. I also asked Sister Caritas, a nun who had been providing me with Bible Study lessons, to look over the chapters. I wanted to make sure that no part of the story was contradictory to the Bible. They all did some minor proofing, but never made any major suggestions. Sometimes they would ask me questions, but usually, they would just say, "When will you have the next chapter available?"

As I was working long hours with my job, it took me months to complete each chapter. After the first four chapters were done, I began searching for a publisher. I was not successful. I continued to get the same response from each of them; "We do not take unsolicited manuscripts." My hopes were dashed.

I began rationalizing that since the little bit of leisure time I had was devoted to writing this book, I was going to quit writing. It just seemed like a waste of time. The other thoughts that kept running through my mind were: "No one is going to want to read this book." "It is a silly idea to even try," "I have no writing talent," "People will mock me for such poor work," "A fifth grader could do a better job." So, sadly, I listened to these voices for four years and put the unfinished book on a shelf.

Toward the end of those four years, Mary said to Duke, in a sad voice, "All of those empty pages." Duke said she was disappointed in me. I realized those discouraging thoughts had not been coming from God. They were attempts to stop the story from ever reaching people who needed to read it, and Satan was winning.

So, between the message from Mary and the encouragement from my rosary group, I got jolted back into writing.

The week I completed the final editing of the final chapter, I saw a pop-up add on Facebook that said, "Publish your Christian book with West Bow Press." I contacted them, drove to visit their offices in Indiana, wrote them a check, and started the process. Since it is a self-publishing company, I will never make money on <u>Through Mary's Eyes</u> or the book you are reading now. I have to pay for any professional editing and artwork myself. Also, I tend to give a lot of books away, so in the end, it costs me much more than I will ever earn. But that doesn't matter, as long as I am doing what Our Lady and Our Lord want me to do. It brings me peace and joy to bring these stories to others.

I have heard about many people who were touched by the book, <u>Through Mary's Eyes</u>, and I hope that this book does the same. I just want people to grow closer to God. It doesn't matter if you are Catholic or not; we all love and honor the same God.

Many times, I have felt a nudge to give a book to a certain person, and wonderful things usually resulted. Once I gave a book to the man who came every six months for my furnace maintenance. Six months after that, he said that both he and his sister had read <u>Through Mary's Eyes</u>, and both were going back to church because of it!

Less than a month after I moved to my new parish in northern Kentucky, I was praying the rosary before a daily mass. The woman leading the rosary seemed to be very devout. I had a nudge to give her my book. I stored some in the trunk of my car, so, after Mass, I met the lady in the parking lot and told her, "I think you are supposed to have this book." Before long, this lady, Pat, who has since become a dear friend, had introduced me to many other members of the parish. I became involved in two prayer groups, the Respect Life Committee, Bible studies, Cursillo, and the Spiritual Motherhood program. My faith is continually being nourished through these connections.

I have received many wonderful reviews of the book. I have included a few here.

The following are cut and pasted from the Amazon site:

LuAnn

5.0 out of 5 stars <u>Used for a women's Bible study.</u>

Reviewed in the United States on December 7, 2019
Verified Purchase

We used this for discussion in a women's Bible study. Although we couldn't find study questions, we enjoyed talking about our love for this story and for our Holy Mother. It gave us lots to think about.

Amazon Customer

5.0 out of 5 stars <u>Five Stars</u>

Reviewed in the United States on April 6, 2018
Verified Purchase
Absolutely fantastic from start to finish!

warry714

5.0 out of 5 stars <u>I love this story!</u>

Reviewed in the United States on September 4, 2012
Verified Purchase
This is the dearest story I have ever read. It touched my heart and soul. You really feel like you are a character in the book. I laughed and cried with the characters.
This is a book that I will share with others and will definitely read again and again.

Connie

5.0 out of 5 stars <u>Mary comes ALIVE! in this book ... .</u>

Reviewed in the United States on April 9, 2014
Verified Purchase
Loved it! Actually, someone let me read their book and I wanted to re-read it again and have my own book to share.

5.0 out of 5 stars <u>Brought Tears of Joy to My Eyes</u>

Reviewed in the United States on January 20, 2018
Brought Tears of Joy to My Eyes and consistent with one of many Biblical mysteries I have wondered for years about - as well as the answer. What happened to Jesus' Mother post his Ascension to Heaven? Why did she have to stay and how could she even feel joy the next several years of her life. Prior to reading this book it became clear Mary was one of the few physical bodies simply brought up and out of this world. The reasoning is obvious. Science or any opportunist would love to have her body or parts of it - and this is why there is no formal burial site for Mary or corpus. The author here, Claire A. Patterson, is fairly exact about how this went down and the story not so far from "religious fiction."
How author Claire A. Patterson depicted Mary's departure made sense and is what brought tears to my eyes. The book also discusses many of the activities around the death of our Lord and Savior - so we can better grasp the importance as well as journey back in time. Thank you, Claire A. Patterson, for researching and writing such a thoughtful book. ~Author Deborah
One person found this helpful

Amazon Customer

5.0 out of 5 stars <u>I cried tears of joy as I relived every part of our Savior's life …</u>

Reviewed in the United States on May 26, 2018
Through Mary's Eyes gives a roadmap for all the mysteries of the rosary. The only story I know that talks about the mother of our Lord and how she fared when He was born, during his childhood, his suffering and death, and resurrection - and final Ascension into heaven. I cried tears of joy as I relived every part of our Savior's life and that of His mother. A MUST read for everyone who wants to know about Our Lady and her purpose for us.

Pat D.

5.0 out of 5 stars <u>A Must Read</u>

Reviewed in the United States on September 25, 2012
I read this beautiful story over a weekend. So much is left unknown in our Bible, but through this author's imagination, we got to travel the rest of Mary's life with her. I've shared this book with many people who have loved it as much as I. Thank you for a beautiful story and a wonderful weekend of reading.

Nichole Cooper (my niece)

5.0 out of 5 stars <u>Excellent!</u>

Reviewed in the United States on June 1, 2012
I thoroughly enjoyed reading this book! I finished it in one day. It is very well written and makes you feel like you are right there with the characters. I recommend everyone read it regardless of religious persuasion.

The following were comments of <u>Through Mary's Eyes</u> sent to me through email or notecards:

"Claire,

I saw my Dad yesterday and he told me he had read your book in two days, which for my Dad is unbelievable. He said when he started reading it, he couldn't put it down. He asked if he could keep it longer and let a friend at church read it. He really enjoyed it. Just wanted to let you know. Have a nice Thanksgiving.

Love, Mary Ann"

"...When I was at bible study Tuesday morning, your name came up because of two people who told about your book; how it fills 'blank spaces' that the Bible doesn't tell us about! And I was thinking that maybe we could arrange a time for you to talk to some of these people about the book. Would that be possible?

Love you guys, Sal"

"Good morning, Claire,

I finished the book you wrote, late last week. I couldn't put it down when I started it. The scourging scene was heart wrenching. But the most significant learning for me was how you presented the real 'human' life of Mary. It has changed how I pray and talk to Mary.

Thank you for this gift, Steve"

My Favorite review, however was from my brother, Jeff.

"Hon,

I wanted to let you know that I read your book today. Let me tell you something to put this statement into perspective. It's extremely rare for me to read an entire book in one day. Actually, it's extremely rare for me to read an entire short story in one day. To be perfectly honest, it's extremely rare for me to read an entire magazine article in one day. Does that give you any clue as to what I think of your book? Have you ever heard the expression, "I couldn't put it down?"

I'm generally a pretty critical and cynical person and not at all liberal with my praises. So, if I told you "I liked your book," that would be a huge compliment coming from me. Well, I have to say that ... I REALLY, REALLY, REALLY enjoyed your book!!

It was definitely thought provoking and very interesting how you wove in your take on some century-long mysteries. But most of all, it was very, very moving.

I especially liked your character, Ruth. Where did you come up with that name to be one of your most endearing characters? (Ruth was our mother's name.)

Love, Jeff"

<u>Through Mary's Eyes</u>, published in 2011, is the book I wrote that incorporates many of the glimpses Duke received. It is a story of Mary's life after Jesus' death, but it also contains flashbacks of her earlier years, as told to the disciples. This book can be purchased through West Bow press, Amazon, or religious bookstores. It is available in hard cover, paperback, and Kindle.

10

Peacocks and Roses

Duke's death was unexpected. He had his last knee surgery on Monday, August 13, 2012. He was scheduled to stay in the hospital until Thursday, but they discharged him early on Wednesday because he was recovering so quickly.

We took our grand-daughter, Ella, (aged seven at that time) to Chuck-E-Cheese on Friday, and Duke came along with his walker. I bought them each a cup of tokens and they had fun teasing each other and stealing tokens from one another's cups. Duke liked to play the games just like Ella did. I enjoyed watching them have so much fun.

On Saturday I took Duke to his first out-patient therapy session. The therapist was very pleased with the way he could bend and stretch his knee. The surgeon had told me that they had achieved an excellent fit. The therapist agreed. Duke was doing very well.

After I got him settled into the house, I went out into the rose garden to weed and spread mulch. An hour later, Chris, our son, came out to the backyard beaming with joy. He told me that he and his father had had a great talk that ended with, "I love you," and hugs. I imagine the Holy Spirit prompted their heartfelt conversation at that time.

On Sunday, August 19, Duke, Chris and I went to Mass. After Mass we stopped at a grocery store to pick up a few things, and Duke and Chris went inside together. Duke was feeling good enough to do a bit of light shopping with his walker.

I had invited my Dad (ninety years old at that time and still driving) over for an early dinner that Sunday, and then he and Duke enjoyed watching a Red's baseball game.

After Dad left, I went into the dining-room to work on a jigsaw puzzle. Chris stayed in the TV room with Duke. I came into the room about an hour later, and found Duke slumped over in his chair. Chris had not noticed anything out of the ordinary, as he was focused on his computer.

I called 911 and they came within five minutes. Chris and I were sent into the living room while they applied the defibrillator paddles. Then they put Duke in an ambulance and Chris and I followed in my car. While I drove to the hospital, Chris left messages for Alicia, our daughter, about what was happening. She and her husband, Michael, were able to join us at the hospital an hour or so later.

It was confusing at the hospital. First one doctor came in and said Duke had a pulse. Then another came in and said he didn't, and that Duke was on life support. The hospital called our parish priest and Duke was given the Sacrament of the Sick about 11:00 p.m. Afterward, Father Jack walked into the waiting room and said to Chris and I, "Didn't I just see you guys at Mass this morning?"

One doctor suggested that we stop the life support and let Duke die that night, but we asked them to run more tests to make sure there was no hope. They said they would.

At some point, I called my brothers and Duke's brother and sister to tell them to meet us back at the hospital the following morning.

Everyone got there about 10:00 a.m. The doctor on duty told us that Duke was brain-dead, and only the machines were keeping him "alive." My brother asked her if she had run the tests as promised, and she said she didn't know. Finally, about 2:30 p.m. they told us there was no hope. Less than ten seconds after the nurse turned off the machine, she looked at me and said, "He's gone."

One of our Marriage Encounter "homework" assignments, years before, had been to write a love letter to our spouse, and tell them what arrangements we would like for our funeral Mass and burial. With that note in hand, making decisions was much easier.

The funeral Mass was beautiful. We were able to select all of Duke's favorite readings, and his favorite flowers. Michael, my dear son-in-law, provided much of the beautiful music that Duke loved.

Duke was buried on Friday, August 24, and the next day, I looked out my kitchen door and saw two peacocks walking around my back yard.

I took pictures and sent them to friends and family. I still don't know the significance of those birds in my yard, but it was pretty amazing and hopeful.

Duke and I had made a pledge to each other years before. We promised that whichever one of us survived the other, he or she would pray for the one who died, to get out of purgatory. Then, when one of us got to heaven, he or she would send a sign. We agreed that the sign would be flowers growing out of season.

As the months went by, Alicia began to mention to me that "Daddy's roses are still blooming." Back then, she would stop by at least once a week to bring Ella over for me to watch, so she mentioned this often throughout October, November and December.

I was still in some kind of haze, because it didn't occur to me to think anything of it. Then one day in December, I looked out of the kitchen door during a snow storm and noticed that the yellow and red roses in our back yard were still blooming. I laughed and imagined Duke and Our Blessed Mother sitting on their rock by the stream, giggling and saying, "How long will it take her to notice?"

Since then, I've studied a lot about Purgatory. I have learned that souls in Purgatory can still reach out and send us messages in many ways. So, there is no guarantee that Duke is in heaven, but we (my son, daughter, and I) have all experienced his presence in one way or another over the years. I still pray for the repose of his soul, and if he is in heaven, he can use my prayers for a soul of his choosing. Prayers are never wasted!

Here are some examples of the ways we have been touched by his presence:

Monday, August 20, two hours before Duke was officially declared dead, we were driving to my bank to retrieve necessary paperwork that was stored in my safety deposit box. During the car ride, Christopher had an experience of which I was not aware at the time. He told me later that he saw and talked to his father. He said he looked younger, healthier, and happy. He wanted Chris to know that he was OK.

A month or so after Duke died, Alicia was thinking about buying a pair of boots she had wanted for a long time. She usually just pushed the desire out of her mind, as they were rather expensive. This time she heard an inner voice saying, "Get your boots, baby. You deserve them." So, she got in her car to drive to the store. Before she turned on the engine, she prayed for a sign to know that the voice was real, and that she wasn't imagining it. As soon as she turned on the car, the radio was playing the Eagles' hit, "Desperado," which was one of Duke's favorite songs.

While we were on a family vacation in August of 2013, approaching the first anniversary of Duke's death, we were eating breakfast all together.

The family vacation photo: left to right: Michael, Ella, Alicia, Chris, Claire

Chris and Alicia both began talking about a very vivid dream they had had that night. Chris said, "All I can say is, I knew he was going to heaven and that the experience was as real as anything else. I mean, I could feel him hug me as if he was still alive and I wasn't dreaming." Alicia said, "We had the same dream!"

Alicia said her father usually gives her a "wink" on his birthday, or her birthday, or another significant date. On June 14, 2016, Duke's birthday, Alicia was pulling something out of a drawer and a photo popped out and landed on the floor. It was this picture of Alicia and Duke dancing at her wedding.

June 20, 2004

In 2016, I had told my granddaughter, Ella, some of the stories I have related here, and she became interested in my rosary that had turned golden. I told her that Our Blessed Mother had been "nudging" me to give it to my friend, Mary Ann, from our original prayer group. Ella said, "Shouldn't it stay in the family?" So, I gave it to Ella. I couldn't shake the feeling, however, that I should have given it to my friend, Mary Ann.

After four months, I told Ella, "I really, really think Our Blessed Mother wants Mary Ann to have that rosary." I arranged a lunch with Mary Ann, Ella and I to present my rosary to her. Mary Ann knew how special the rosary was, and resisted taking it, but I insisted it was for her.

Then, she told us about her mother's rosary. It had turned golden after a blessing from Mary, and then been given to her brother when her mother died. We all agreed that it was Our Blessed Mother's wish that Mary Ann have my special golden rosary.

During the drive home, after that lunch, I promised Ella that she could have my grandfather's rosary, that had been stored in my cedar chest. This chest had been one of Mom's favorite possessions, and after my father died, my brothers agreed that I should have it. I had been through that chest a few times and thought I knew just where to find everything. The first small box I opened, thinking it contained my Grandfather's brown wooden rosary, contained an identical rosary that we had just given to Mary Ann a few hours before! I had never seen that rosary in the cedar chest before. Our Blessed Mother gave me (and Ella) an incredible gift that day!

I supposed my Mom had purchased two identical rosaries in 1974. She gave one to me and kept one for herself. God picked this singular time to have me discover mom's rosary! This rosary, however, still has all silver links. I gave Ella my grandfather's rosary that day, called Mary Ann and we scheduled another lunch to compare our two rosaries.

Here they are side by side.

By the way, I have promised Ella my mother's rosary, if it ever turns golden. So far it has not! I still need to work harder to please our Lady and Jesus!

When Alicia and Michael experienced a house fire in October 2016, they lost 90 percent of their belongings. The electrical fire had started in Ella's bedroom, and she lost almost all of her things. What she did not lose, in that intense heat, was her bible and her Great-great-grandfather's wooden rosary.

They lived in a small condo for eight months while their house was being rebuilt and their smoke damaged items were being treated. They moved back into their house on June 14, 2017, Duke's birthday. The first box of the treated items they opened, out of about a hundred boxes, was the one containing Duke's belongings; among them, his gardening shoes, and one of his rosaries.

In 2017, I gave Alicia my "Our Lady of Grace" garden statue. She had created a space for it surrounded by some of Duke's favorite flowers. When she first put the statue there, Ella saw a beautiful butterfly land on a flower next to the statue. Perhaps this was Duke, and Our Blessed Mother, letting us know they liked the statue there.

Ella is hugging the beautiful statue of Our Lady of Grace in July 2006.

On Mother's Day, 2019, Alicia bought a climbing yellow rose bush. The first yellow bloom opened on Alicia's birthday. Duke always loved roses, and grew them in every yard we ever owned.

Alicia said that on June 20, 2020, Alicia and Michael's wedding anniversary, they were taking a walk and noticed a strong scent of roses. There were no rosebushes in sight. Again, she thought her father was sending her a wink.

After Duke died, I searched endlessly for his rosary that had turned golden after our trip to Medjugorje. Before giving his clothes away, I checked every pocket. I never found it. In early 2020, my son was going through his own belongings and discovered it. I don't remember giving it to Chris, but I am very glad he has it.

Because of Our Blessed Mother's constant love, Jesus' bottomless mercy, St. Michael's protection, St. Joseph's fatherly guidance, and the Holy Spirit's constant stream of Grace, our lives were turned around 180 degrees.

It is hard to imagine what our paths would have been like, had Mary not spoken to Duke that first time on July 3, 2001. Satan might have prevailed and we would have found our marriage a sham or torn asunder. I might be living in fear now, rather than in peace and joy. I have so much gratitude for the many blessings poured out upon us by God, that I am crying tears of joy as I write these words.

Thank you, Lord!

I pray that God blesses you and your loved ones as you read this book, and may it bring you peace, hope and joy.

Final Words of Love

Private message from Our Lady on 9/8/01.

"My Angel,

As always, I send you my motherly love and blessings. Your prayers and fasting have not gone unnoticed. Thank you for your devotion. When you are praying and you feel my presence deeply it is because I am amongst you. When my children are praying from the heart, one of my greatest joys is saying the "Our Father" and the "Glory Be" with them. I tell you the truth, my angel, mankind does not fully recognize the power of prayer. When you pray from the heart, prayer is the greatest force in all of God's creation! Today is the day that has been chosen to honor my birth. As do all mothers, my heart yearns for my children's love and devotion, but the greatest gift that my children could give me is to consecrate their hearts to my Son!"

This photo was taken by my friend, Alice, as we were sitting in the back of St. James Church in Medjugorje. It was during an apparition, and before the evening Coratian mass. It was 9/8/17; the date the church celebrates Mary's birthday. Notice the image of rose petals surrounding the sun. In the colored photo they appear red.

Private message to Duke from our Lady on 10/11/01.

"I send you my love and blessings … Now, more than ever, I need your prayers for peace. Satan is strong and he is mounting a massive offensive against mankind. The world is in great peril. Pray, pray, pray for world peace!"

Duke reported to me that he had received the following private message from our Lady on 12/25/01. He said that Mary appeared in a white gown trimmed in gold. She cradled the baby Jesus in her arms as she spoke.

"My Angel,

Still, so many of my children do not heed my messages. What more can I do or say? They continue to lead lives without meaning. They continue to refuse to heed my messages. The Holy Spirit is striving to lead mankind's hearts toward salvation, but so many of their hearts are made of stone. As long as God allows, through His grace and mercy, I shall continue to strive to lead my children toward greater holiness. I will never tire. I will never cease."

Our Lady's message for "all who will listen" on 1/4/02

"...I call you 'My little children' for a reason. As Jesus has said, 'You must become as little children to enter into the kingdom of heaven.' Most believe that this means that you must be as pure and innocent as little children, and that is true, but it also means so very much more. As little children depend on their parents for all of their needs, you also must depend upon the Father for all of your physical, emotional, and spiritual needs. Little children, have the utmost trust and faith that their parents will provide these needs. So, too, must you have total faith and trust in your heavenly Father. Little children look to their parents for guidance. My little ones, let God lead you in your every action. Little children love their parents with an unconditional love. Your Father in heaven loves you with an unconditional love that surpasses all understanding. Return and reflect the love to the Father and to all that you meet ..."

Duke's rose garden, dedicated to Mary, his loving Mother

Duke was given the following private message from Mary on 1/30/02.

"My Angel,

Do not be overly concerned with the things of this world. They are Satan's greatest snare, and can never provide true happiness. They are fleeting and false; like sand that slips between your fingers. What can this feeble life provide compared to eternity?

Instead, store up your treasures in heaven. Strive constantly toward greater holiness. Pray for the Holy Spirit to transform your hearts. My angel, tell my children to be kind to each other. Pray for love to conquer hate. In your every action and deed, share the love of Christ Jesus..."

This is the transcript of an email I sent out on 5/23/02:

"We had a very special rosary last night. I wish you all could have been there. The minute we made the sign of the cross to begin [praying], I felt Mary's presence. It was like a shock wave. Several others felt it as well. She stayed with us throughout the rosary and spoke to Duke during the fourth glorious mystery. [Mary's Assumption into Heaven].

Her message contained a few points: how happy she was to see so many praying together (we had 15), she extended her motherly love and blessings upon all of us, she blessed religious articles and even those of a man who wasn't with us, and she said that it is up to us, her children, to spread the news that her Son loves us and wants us in heaven. She said she is counting on us to help her. It was a beautiful, beautiful evening.

The peace of that hour is still with me. Love, Claire"

The last message that Duke received from Jesus was given on Friday, 3/30/12 at 3:00 pm, the time of His death on Calvary.

"My Beloved Little Brother,

The world is teetering on the edge of a dark and dismal abyss. The Holy Spirit is continually calling to your hearts for conversion and yet you have turned your hearts to stone. Never before in the history of mankind has the Father been so shunned and denied.

Lucifer has blinded you with his false promises. You have been bombarded by evil for so long that you have become numb. You accept the world that you live in as being 'normal'. So many of my brothers and sisters are existing in a living hell and they don't even realize the conditions around them as being the results of submitting to Satan's will.

I love each soul on earth with a love that has no boundaries. I laid down my life for you! What greater love is there? Come to Me and experience my love and peace. Walk with Me. Talk to Me. Let Me be your greatest advocate. I will wrap you in My cloak and hold you close and protect you against all evil. Lay down your burdens and I will give you rest.

The world is about to enter an era of great tribulation. Behind closed doors alliances are being made. Forces are being gathered for the final battle between good and evil.

You must prepare yourselves to be spiritually upright and strong. You should commit Ephesians 6:11-18 to memory. Our Blessed Mother has given you an arsenal of weapons to prepare for the time ahead. Live her messages! Ask yourselves, 'Why would the Father grant Our Blessed Mother the grace to be with us for such a period of time if it wasn't deemed critical for her to do so?' Wake up, my brothers and sisters! Do not be as the foolish virgins! I tell you the truth, my beloved, I have done and I am continuing to do everything that I possibly can to ensure your salvation!

Our Blessed Mother has asked all of her children to do the following so that they should grow in spirituality: 1) prayer, 2) fast, 3) go to Mass as often as possible, 4) receive the Eucharist with reverence, 5) study the Holy Scriptures, 6) go to confession often, 7) say the rosary daily.

To this, my beloved, I would only add, love one another as I have loved you. Love the Father with all of your heart and soul. Be kind to one another and stand strong in your faith.

All Glory, Praise and Honor be to the Father now and forever. Amen."

Endnotes

1. p. 37 Duke and I had been discussing the Holy Spirit hours before this message was given. It was more evidence that Mary was very present in our lives, even when we weren't aware of her listening in. Another time we were in bed talking and Duke said he felt that Mary was going to give him an important message in the next couple of days. Then she spoke to him immediately and said, "It will come on the fifteenth of this month." My first reaction was, "She is right here, listening to us talk! So, we better be loving and sweet to each other, right?" My second reaction was to run down to the refrigerator calendar and check out the date. August 15 is the feast of her Assumption! Shortly after this, we were leaving Sunday Mass, and as I passed a statue of the Holy Family, I leaned in and kissed baby Jesus' toes. When we got into our car, Duke told me that Mary had just spoken to him. He was told to share with me that Our Blessed Mother used to love to kiss baby Jesus' toes also. These were such special, tender moments!

2. p. 38 Duke loved that she called him "My Angel." He thought it was so special.

3. p. 39 During the rosary the night before, Duke had told me how much he missed Mary.

4. p. 41 Several years later, we were at Our Lady of the Holy Spirit Center and I was looking through items on the "free" table. I saw a book of the saints. It reminded me of the one my mom owned as I was growing up. I grabbed this new-found treasure and took it home. When I opened it, I saw "Raymond Favret" written on the first page. My guess is that after he died, the church donated his books to the OLHSC library. I think Father Ray was winking at us from heaven!

5. p. 43 When I was in high school, I learned about the church in the middle ages. Many church leaders were corrupt, and sold indulgences to the poor to build cathedrals and increase their personal wealth. I became cynical of the idea of purgatory, thinking that the greedy church leaders just made up the idea in order to enrich their coffers. It wasn't until Duke's conversation with Mary about my mom's experience in purgatory, that I believed it was true. Then I felt terribly guilty that I hadn't had masses said for her or prayed for the repose of her soul. I have no way of knowing how long she was there, but I pray each day, now, for the souls in Purgatory.

6. p. 46 I did finally see a miracle of the sun during my third trip to Medjugorje, in May 2019. I was sitting on a bench alone, waiting for the outside Mass to begin, and just turned my head to the left. I noticed that I could look at the sun without burning my eyes. It was a white disc; no colors or movements, but I felt very peaceful and blessed. I did not share this with anyone at the time. Afterwards, I began to worry because I had stared at the sun for at least ten minutes. I thought that I might have done permanent damage to my eyes, but I was just fine.

7. p. 50 It is a tradition that has been occurring since the 1850's. Mary called Immaculata Church her "Church on the Hill." It is a very special place for many Catholics in Cincinnati.

8. p. 57 Before this message, we had been fasting from midnight to midnight. We found that fasting from sundown to sundown was much healthier and easier to manage.

9. p. 58 This is the quote from Holy Scripture that my children and I decided to put on the back of the prayer card for Duke's funeral Mass.

10. p. 60 I remember teasing Duke that Father Slavko was only fifty-four years old when he died. That was only three years older than Duke was at that time. "Was he really an old man?" I asked. Duke said, "Well he looked old. He had white hair and a lot of wrinkles."

CPSIA information can be obtained
at www.ICGtesting.com
Printed in the USA
LVHW010219081220
673553LV00007B/1247